BUILD YOUR OWN
PAPER ROBOTS

BUILD YOUR OWN
PAPER ROBOTS

JULIUS PERDANA AND
JOSH BUCZYNSKI

WITH
AXEL BERNAL
ELSO LÓPEZ
ARIF SUSENO
KURT YOUNG

I L E X

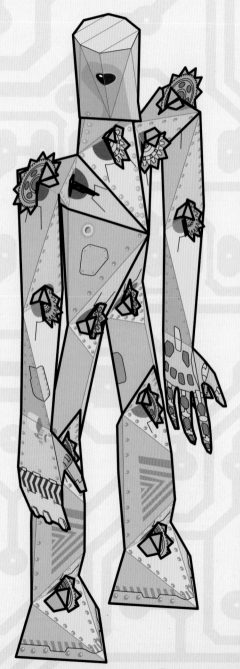

First published in the United Kingdom
in 2010 by:

I L E X

210 High Street
Lewes
East Sussex
BN7 2NS
www.ilex-press.com

Publisher: Alastair Campbell
Creative Director: Peter Bridgewater
Managing Editor: Nick Jones
Editor: Ellie Wilson
Commissioning Editor: Tim Pilcher
Art Director: Julie Weir
Designers: Jon Allan and Ginny Zeal
Technical Editor: Nick Rowland

British Library Cataloguing-in-Publication Data
A catalogue record for this book is available from
the British Library.

ISBN 978-1-907579-01-1

Printed and bound in China

Colour Origination by Ivy Press Reprographics.

10 9 8 7 6 5 4 3 2 1

CONTENTS

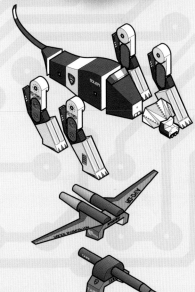

Introduction

Build Your Own Paper Robots provides you with 12 professionally designed paper robots, and two paper backgrounds to act as display stands for your robots. Whether you are an experienced papercrafter or new to the hobby there is a model to suit you: from comical designs to the fantastical.

If you are just starting out in the world of papercraft, try one of the simpler models first, such as Chompybot or Dogbot, and work your way up to the monsters like Spiderbot!

If you would like to customize any of the robots to your own tastes, the files on the CD allow you to digitally color your own design onto one of the robots' templates, or you can print out the linework and traditionally color it in.

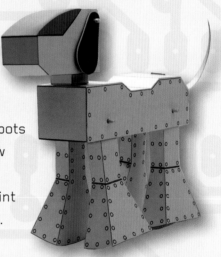

Key:

| Score | Cut | Glue | Rubber band | Sewing needle |

Folding tips: The robots use a combination of valley folds and mountain folds.

A mountain fold is made as if you were opening a book, stretching it back so the "covers" touch—like a mountain ridge.

A valley fold is made as if you were closing a book—so the sheet becomes a valley.

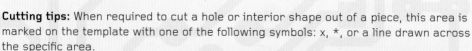

Cutting tips: When required to cut a hole or interior shape out of a piece, this area is marked on the template with one of the following symbols: x, *, or a line drawn across the specific area.

What you will need

Using the right tools for the job will help you immensely when building the models supplied with this book. Some of the models are very intricate, and will need extra time and care taken to cut them out precisely and glue them together firmly.

General tools:

1. Paper: Thin card, like a business card or double-sided matte card that is around 200-220gsm.

2. Glue: PVA glue, also known as "white glue." Some modelers use UHU glue (or another brand with similar properties). Pick a glue that is strong, fast-acting, and creates minimal mess.

3. A craft knife: Craft knives or modeling knives are best for small, intricate cuts.

4. Scissors: Sharp scissors can be easier to use for cutting along curved lines.

5. Cutting mat: To help you make smooth cuts in the paper and protect your workspace underneath.

6. Ruler: Ideally a metal ruler, for cutting and scoring along paper folds.

7. Scorer: This can be the blunt edge of a craft knife, or a dead ballpoint pen.

Handy tools:

1. Q-tips: For cleaning up excess glue. You will need to dampen the ends first so the cotton does not stick to the glue.

2. Glue applicator: Toothpick for tricky areas and a paintbrush (or something similar) for larger parts.

3. Tweezers: Handy for the small, intricate bits and holding the pieces together while the glue dries.

Specific tools for individual models:

SPIDERBOT AND TANKBOT

1. Rubber bands or wire.

2. Staple pins: Pierce these through the rubber band and use as a "needle" to thread through the holes.

3. Coffee stirrers or plastic straws to use as supports for the joints.

MEDEVAC, LIONBOT, BLAZEFIGHTER, AND CONSTRUCTOR

4. Balsa wood.

DOGBOT

5. Toothpicks.

MICROBOT

6. Scotch tape for disk joints.

CONSTRUCTOR

7. Clear plastic sheet.

What's on the disc

The disc on the front of this book contains all the templates you need to make your own paper robots and backgrounds. These have been designed so they are ideal for printing at home on your inkjet printer, on Letter- or A4-sized paper (or larger). As well as printing out full color templates, there are also blank templates on the disc that you can color yourself— either on your computer, or after you've printed the template out.

We'll look at printing and coloring your templates on the following pages, but for now let's take a quick look at what's on the disc, and where you can find it.

The opening screen of the disc contains a *License Agreement* and two folders for the *Robots* and *Backgrounds*. You must read and agree to the license before using any image on the disc. To make any one of the 12 robots featured in this book, open the *Robots* folder (or the *Backgrounds* folder if you want to make a background).

Inside the Robots folder you'll find the 12 individual robots waiting for you—just double-click on the one you want.

The Letter and A4 sub-folders contain templates that have been designed for printing on either Letter or A4 paper, so make sure you open the right one for your printer.

Inside each of the paper size folders are a final two folders—*Color* and *Line Art*. These contain the templates themselves.

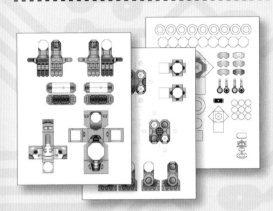

The Color templates for each robot have been saved as a single PDF file, which means you can open it using Adobe Reader (or a similar program) and print out all of the pages you need to build a single robot. Reader is installed with most operating systems, but if you haven't got it on your computer (or a program that will read PDF files) you can download it for free from www.adobe.com. We'll look at how to print out the color templates on the following pages.

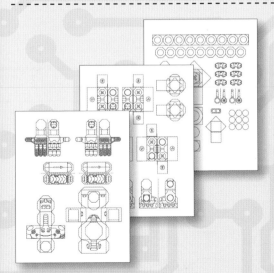

The Line Art templates are PSD files rather than a single PDF file, so you can color them easily in an image-editing program. Depending on the robot or background that you've chosen there could be several files to open and you need to open and color them all for each robot.

The PSD files can be opened using a wide range of image-editing programs, including Adobe Photoshop, Photoshop Elements, and Corel Paint Shop Pro. If you don't already have software on your computer that will open the PSD files you can download a trial version of any of these programs. Alternatively you can download a free image-editing program called Gimp from www.gimp.org, which is perfect for working on your robots.

Printing Color Templates

All of the robots in this book have been supplied as fully colored templates on the disc, so all you need to do is open the color PDF file for your chosen robot, and print it out. The PDF template file contains all the pages you need to build one robot, which could be anything from two pages to 20 pages, so before you start printing, make sure you've got enough card to print all the pages. If you have, then use the following steps to guide you through the printing process.

Page Setup

The color templates have been sized to fit either Letter or A4 paper, and it's important that you check your printer's settings to make sure the pages print properly. In Adobe Reader, choose *File > Page Setup* from the top menu to open the Page Setup dialog window.

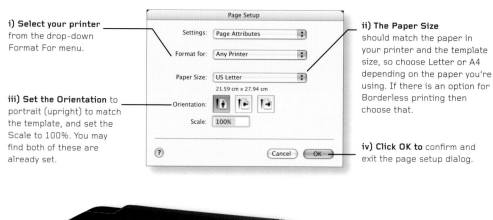

i) Select your printer from the drop-down Format For menu.

ii) The Paper Size should match the paper in your printer and the template size, so choose Letter or A4 depending on the paper you're using. If there is an option for Borderless printing then choose that.

iii) Set the Orientation to portrait (upright) to match the template, and set the Scale to 100%. You may find both of these are already set.

iv) Click OK to confirm and exit the page setup dialog.

Page Setup
Settings: Page Attributes
Format for: Any Printer
Paper Size: US Letter
21.59 cm x 27.94 cm
Orientation:
Scale: 100%
Cancel   OK

Print

Printers use a dialog window called a "driver" to control them, and every manufacturer uses a different system. The accompanying illustration is for a Canon printer, so your printer driver might look a bit different. However, all of the settings we'll be changing can be found in every printer driver— if you can't find them, take a look in the printer's manual or help file on your computer. To access the Print window, choose *File > Print* from the Adobe Reader top menu. The following settings are the ones you need to find and check:

Print All: Make sure you are printing all of the pages in the template, not just the current one, or a selection.

Page Scaling: If you set your printer to Borderless printing in the Page Setup dialog then the template will fit perfectly on the page.

If your printer doesn't allow Borderless printing, choose Fit to Printable Area instead. This will mean that none of the pieces on the template will be cut off by your printer.

Media Type: Set the media type to Plain Paper if you are using plain card stock that isn't specifically designed for inkjet printers. This will stop you using too much ink when you print the template.

If you are using a more expensive inkjet card, then check on the packet what you should set your printer to.

Providing you set these three options you should be ready to print, so press Print and your template(s) should be ready for you to construct your very first paper robot.

SCALING UP

Although the robot templates come in Letter and A4 sizes, there's no reason why you can't make your robots bigger. If you own a large format printer that will let you print on Tabloid or A3 paper, you can use that instead. Just be sure to select the larger paper size in your printer driver when you want to print the template out, and choose Fit to Page. This will enlarge the template to fit the larger paper size, so you can make giant robots!

If you don't have a large format printer at home, you could print out a set of Letter- or A4-sized templates and take those to your local copy store. Most copy stores can enlarge from Letter to Tabloid, or A4 to A3. They might not be able to copy onto card, but don't let that stop you—copy them onto paper and then stick that to thin card before cutting the pieces out and making your robot.

Coloring Line Art Templates

The Line Art folder on the disc contains a set of blank templates for every robot and background for you to color—either on your computer, or using pens, pencils, or paint. If you want to color the blank files using pens or pencils, then you can jump straight to the printing section (see box bottom of page 15) to print out a set of blank templates.

However, if you want to color them on your computer, the following tips and tricks will help you out.

Simple Fill

The Line Art templates come in the form of PSD files, and all of the robots (except Chompybot) and backgrounds use two or more files—you need to color and print them all to make a whole robot! We're using Photoshop here, but you can use Photoshop Elements, Paint Shop Pro, or even Gimp to color your robots. Be aware, however, that some of the tools might be called a different name.

1. Start by opening all of the pages for your chosen robot in your editing program. The pages are saved on the disc as Grayscale images, so the first step is to convert the files to color. In Photoshop, choose *Image > Mode > RGB* from the top menu. If asked, don't flatten the image.

- -

2. Next, open the Layers palette in your editing program. You will see that the files are supplied as two separate layers—the top one (Layer 1) is the outline of the pieces, and the bottom one is a plain white background. Click on the outline layer as this is the one we want to color.

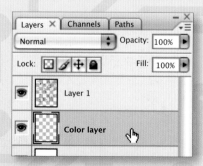

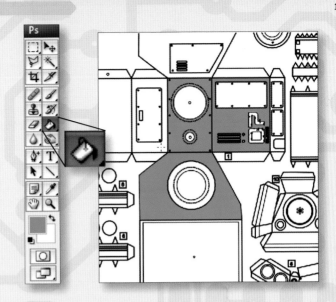

3. To add solid colors to the different parts of the template, select the Paint Bucket tool from the Toolbar and click inside the area of the template that you want to color. Because the template sections have solid outlines, the area you click on will be filled with color.

4. You can change the color in Photoshop and Photoshop Elements by double-clicking on the foreground color square in the Toolbar. This will open the Color Picker, where you can click to select a different color for the Paint Bucket tool to use.

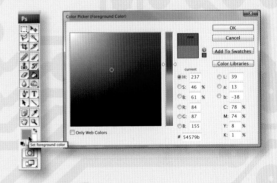

5. Keep changing colors and filling the areas of the template until you are done. Remember to color all the pages before printing them!

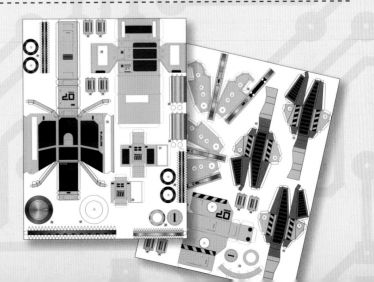

Coloring Line Art Templates (cont.)

Although the Paint Bucket tool is a great way of quickly coloring a template, it limits you to flat blocks of color. For some robots this might be all you want, but if you reach for the Brush tool instead, you can start getting a little more creative.

1. As before, start by converting the template into a color, RGB file and then open the Layers palette. Instead of selecting the outline layer, select the background layer and then add a new layer (*Layer > New > Layer*). The new layer will now appear between the existing layers—call it Color layer.

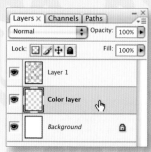

2. The reason we added the new color layer is so we can paint on it without coloring over the template. So pick the Brush tool from the Toolbar and start work.

3. The Brush tool works just like a paintbrush. Your editing program will let you adjust the size, shape, and hardness of the brush, and you can change the paint color by double-clicking the foreground color as before.

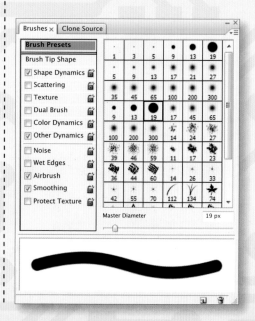

4. You can now paint your template "freehand" rather than adding blocks of flat color. You could use different colors to create a camouflage pattern, or use lighter and darker shades of the same color to add highlights and shadows. Because you're working on a layer beneath the template outline there's no risk of losing the important cutting and folding lines, and don't worry if you go outside the lines of the template—when you've printed your template you will cut these areas out to make your robot.

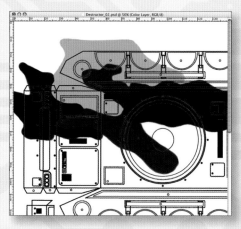

5. Keep painting the template until you're done, remembering to paint all the pages for the robot you want to build before printing it out and building your own, unique robot. Why not try using similar paint-schemes for several robots to build a mecha army?

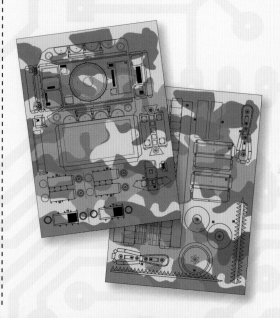

PRINTING YOUR COLORED LINE ART TEMPLATES

Printing your templates out follows the same steps as printing out the pre-colored templates, but because the blank templates are supplied as a series of individual files, it's very important that you use the same settings to print each page. The most crucial setting is Scaling. If your printer has a Borderless printing option, print ALL of the files Borderless. If it doesn't have this option, make sure you print ALL the files at the same size using the Fit To Page option, or by setting the scaling to 95% in the printer driver window. This will make sure that all the templates are the same size, so all the pieces match when you build your robot.

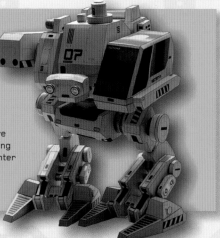

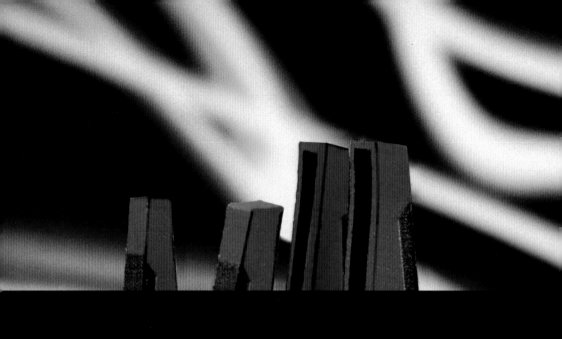

ROBOTS

CHOMPYBOT

FIREPOWER

STRENGTH

MANEUVERABILITY

ARMOR

INTELLIGENCE

The Chompybot comes in three different designs—a social robot that is more at ease in groups. This type of robot is not equipped with weapons for attack, however its robust body shell and powerful clamping jaws provide ample protection. Large hands improve clamping leverage and its deep mouth chasm is perfect for storing mechanical food. Large, fully rotational eyes give the Chompybot heightened sight capabilities, although, due to a lack of intelligence, it can often throw the bot off balance and accounts for a somewhat goofy appearance.

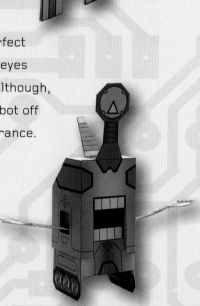

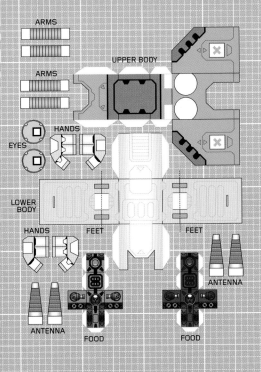

ARMS

UPPER BODY

ARMS

EYES

HANDS

LOWER BODY

HANDS

FEET FEET

ANTENNA

ANTENNA FOOD FOOD

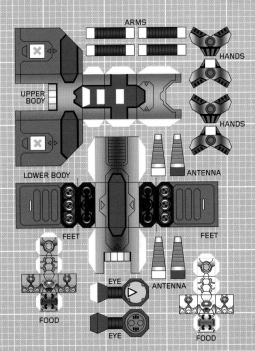

ARMS

UPPER BODY

HANDS

HANDS

ANTENNA

LOWER BODY

FEET FEET

EYE

FOOD ANTENNA

EYE FOOD

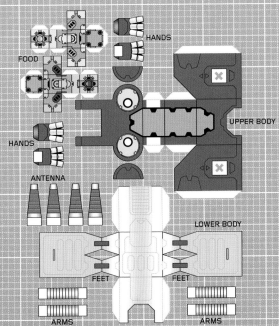

FOOD

HANDS

HANDS

UPPER BODY

ANTENNA

LOWER BODY

FEET FEET

ARMS ARMS

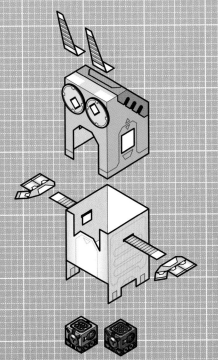

1 Cut and fold all the pieces. Also cut out all the interior shapes marked with "x."

2 Starting with the lower body (base), score along the lines and fold. Assemble the lower body shape, gluing the tabs and the feet together.

3 Fold and stick the arms to the lower body through the slots.

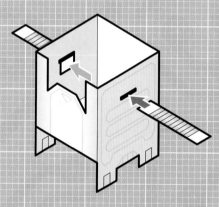

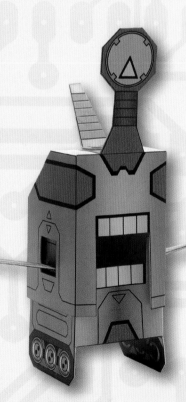

4 Score and fold the main body (upper body or head) and glue together, using the tabs.

5 Slide the lower body into the upper body, making sure the arms go through the holes on the upper body.

7 Add the finishing touches. Glue on the eyes, hands, and the antennae, et volia!

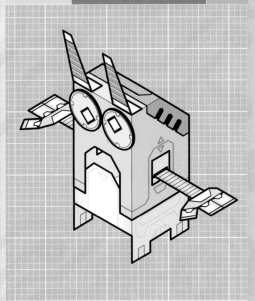

6 Assemble the cubes by gluing the corresponding tabs together. These are Chompybot's energy sources—his mechanical food.

LIONBOT

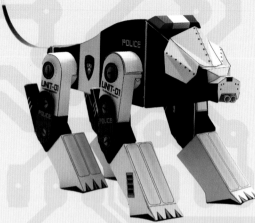

FIREPOWER

STRENGTH

MANEUVERABILITY

ARMOR

INTELLIGENCE

Lionbot is the most versatile of this robot group. A highly specialized machine, Lion is a valuable member of crime fighting, ambush, and recovery teams. With two interchangeable add-ons, Lion can be customized to meet the demands of most battle situations. Armed with mouth guns, police lights, and a head shield, Lion can change between bazooka guns and rocket-powered wings giving him an aerial advantage as well as a powerful arsenal. The highly sophisticated robot armor is bulletproof and fireproof, making this an ideal attack and defense weapon like no other.

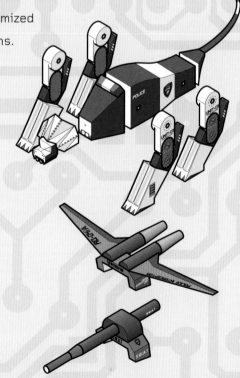

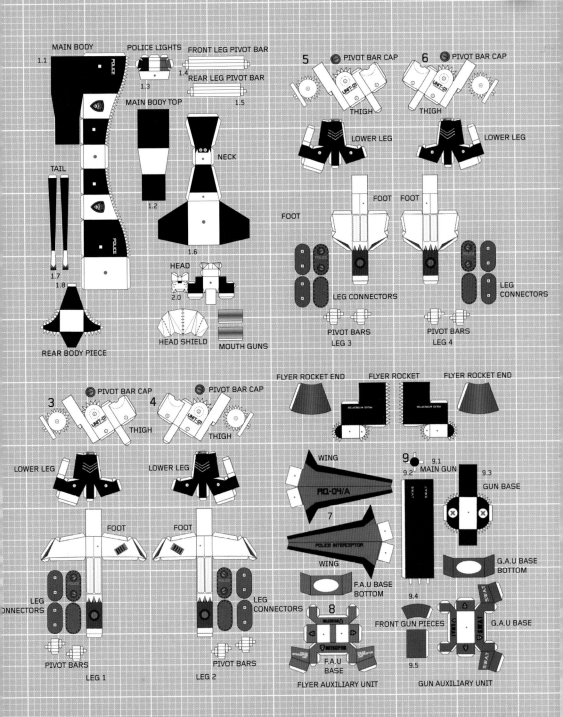

1

Cut out and score all the pieces for the head.

2

Carefully fold along the scored lines, using both mountain and valley folds for the head shield, and assemble the head by gluing the tabs. Coil the mouth guns around something cylindrical and glue all the head components together.

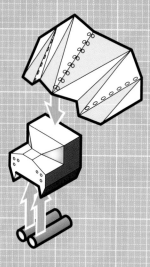

3

Cut, score, fold, and assemble the leg pieces, gluing the tabs. Remember to only cut out all the interior shapes marked with a red "x."

4

Glue the leg connectors together and glue the pivot bars to one side of the connector. Insert the pivot bars in the holes on the lower leg and thigh pieces and then close by gluing the free ends of the pivot bars to the second connector. Glue the lower leg to the foot piece.

5

Repeat for the other front leg and the two hind legs.

* Note: If you find the pivot bars are too fiddly to make, you can try covering a stick of balsa wood with some card paper and cutting it to size.

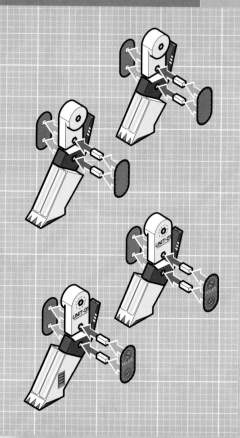

6

Cut, score, and fold the body parts. Remember to only cut out the little boxes marked with a red "x." Glue together using the tabs. Also cut out the tail. Curl the tail around your finger or a cylindrical object to make it curl upwards.

7

Assemble the main body parts, gluing the pieces together. Insert the front and rear leg pivot bars through the pivot bar holes.

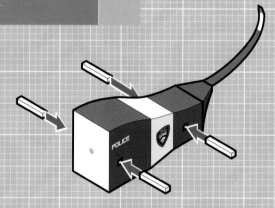

8

Attach the legs to the body using the pivot bars and glue the connector circle to cover the joint.

9

Assemble the neck piece, gluing the tabs, and glue the head to the neck. Glue the neck to the main body.

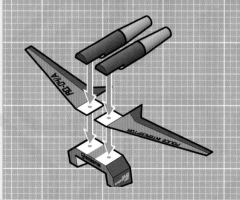

10

Cut, score, fold, and glue the pieces for the Flyer Auxiliary unit.

11

Glue the flyer rocket to the wing pieces and glue the wings to the wing main body.

12

Cut, score, fold, and glue the pieces for the Gun Auxiliary unit.

13

Glue the front three gun pieces together and then glue to the gun main unit. Then attach the fourth rear gun piece.

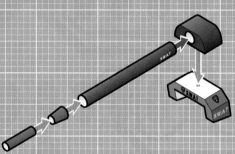

14

Do not glue the auxiliary units to the main body of Lionbot; these can be attached and detached for different display options.

✔

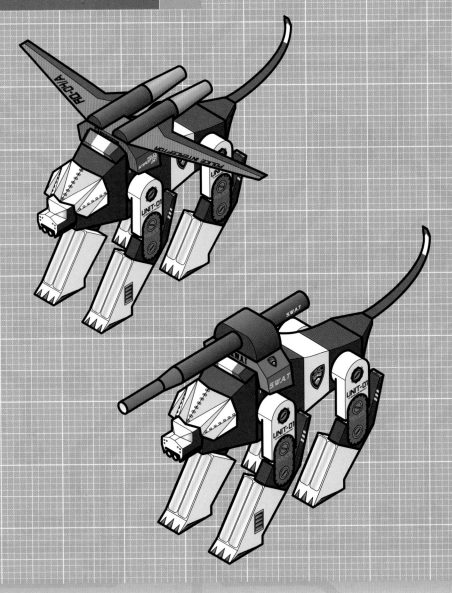

MICROBOT

FIREPOWER

STRENGTH

MANEUVERABILITY

ARMOR

INTELLIGENCE

The engineer's robot, Microbot has all the skills and tools to fix the most complicated technical problems. As cool as its carbon-metal suit of armor, Microbot's colored shades equip the bot with X-ray vision for identifying mechanical malfunctions. Fully rotational hips allow Microbot easy access to most nooks and crannies, and facilitate its capacity for speed as well as flexibility. He is available in different color schemes.

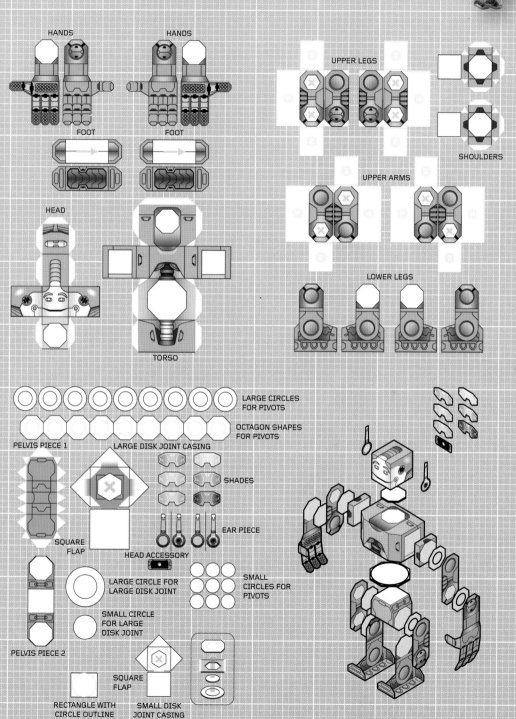

HANDS

HANDS

UPPER LEGS

SHOULDERS

FOOT

FOOT

UPPER ARMS

HEAD

LOWER LEGS

TORSO

LARGE CIRCLES
FOR PIVOTS

OCTAGON SHAPES
FOR PIVOTS

PELVIS PIECE 1

LARGE DISK JOINT CASING

SHADES

EAR PIECE

SQUARE
FLAP

HEAD ACCESSORY

LARGE CIRCLE FOR
LARGE DISK JOINT

SMALL
CIRCLES FOR
PIVOTS

SMALL CIRCLE
FOR LARGE
DISK JOINT

PELVIS PIECE 2

SQUARE
FLAP

RECTANGLE WITH
CIRCLE OUTLINE

SMALL DISK
JOINT CASING

1 Glue hands, arms, feet, and legs to a blank sheet of card so that it is double the thickness. Leave aside to dry.

2 Cut out and score the pieces for the head, torso, and pelvis.

3 Assemble the head and torso, gluing the tabs.

4 Assemble the two pelvis pieces together, gluing the bottom piece to the top piece.

5 Cover the backs of the large circles for the pivots with Scotch tape and then cut them out. Cut out all the small circles and glue them to the centers of the larger ones.

6 Next, work on the two disk joints for the head and torso. Cut away the six-sided shape from inside the disk casing and tape over the inside of the square flap. Place, but do not glue, the large circle underneath the casing, so the smaller one sits in the hole.

7 Fold over the square flap so it covers the back of the large circle. Glue it closed using the triangle tabs of the casing, let it dry, then cut off the corners.

8 For the large disk joint, glue the rectangle with the circle outline to the small circle in the casing. For the small disk joint, glue the octagon shaped pivot piece to the small circle in the small disk casing.

9 Don't let the glue touch the edges of the casing or your pivot will not work. Allow to dry, then twist to ensure the circle spins within the disk casing.Cut, score, and fold the shoulder pieces, and assemble, gluing the tabs.

10

Glue the shoulders to the torso. Glue small pivot to the head and large pivot to torso. Now glue the head, torso, and pelvis to each other.

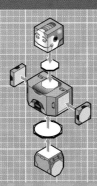

13

Cut out the holes from the upper legs and assemble the pivots as before, putting tape on the back of the flap marked 1. Repeat for arms, but only put tape on the back half of both the flaps marked 1, where the disk joints sit.

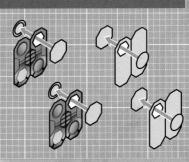

11

Cut out the pieces for the foot. Score, fold, and glue them together (they should now be four sheets thick). Score again, so that the toe and the heel can bend upwards.

14

Glue both hand pieces together and then score and cut to separate the fingers and bend inward.

15

Assemble arms and legs and glue to the shoulders and hip respectively.

12

Glue the lower leg pieces together leaving bottom flaps unglued and separated to be a flat base. Glue this to the foot piece gluing the heel and toe to the front and back of the leg piece.

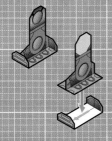

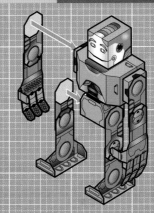

MEDEVAC

FIREPOWER

STRENGTH

MANEUVERABILITY

ARMOR

INTELLIGENCE

Medevac is designed to provide
first-response medical assistance
in any emergency and is equipped
with a radio helmet and a chemical
backpack of self-replenishing medical
supplies. His long legs give him exceptional
speed and added to this are the rotor blades
on Medevac's arms enabling him to fly and
hover. Medevac's sleek and slim design
makes him especially aerodynamic so that
he can reach emergencies and rescue
sites quicker than ordinary helicopters.

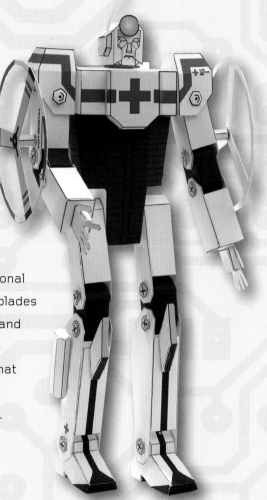

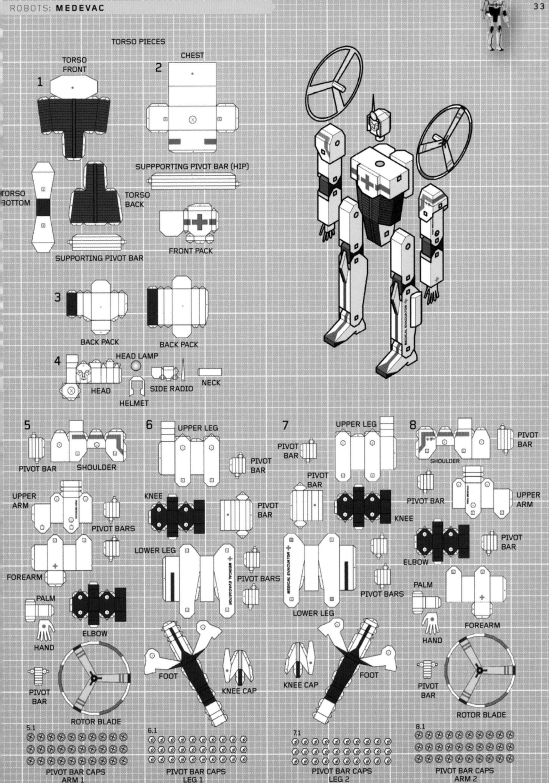

TORSO PIECES

1 TORSO FRONT

2 CHEST

SUPPPORTING PIVOT BAR (HIP)

TORSO BOTTOM

TORSO BACK

SUPPORTING PIVOT BAR

FRONT PACK

3 BACK PACK

BACK PACK

4 HEAD LAMP

HEAD

HELMET

SIDE RADIO

NECK

5 PIVOT BAR SHOULDER

UPPER ARM

PIVOT BARS

FOREARM

PALM

ELBOW

HAND

PIVOT BAR

ROTOR BLADE

5.1 PIVOT BAR CAPS ARM 1

6 UPPER LEG

PIVOT BAR

KNEE

PIVOT BAR

LOWER LEG

PIVOT BARS

FOOT

KNEE CAP

6.1 PIVOT BAR CAPS LEG 1

7 UPPER LEG

PIVOT BAR

PIVOT BAR

KNEE

MEDICAL EVACUATOR

PIVOT BARS

LOWER LEG

KNEE CAP

FOOT

7.1 PIVOT BAR CAPS LEG 2

8 PIVOT BAR

SHOULDER

PIVOT BAR

UPPER ARM

PIVOT BAR

ELBOW

PALM

HAND

FOREARM

PIVOT BAR

ROTOR BLADE

8.1 PIVOT BAR CAPS ARM 2

1 Cut, score, and fold the pieces for the head, helmet, headlamp, and neck, cutting out all the interior shapes marked with an "x."

2 Assemble the head, gluing the small tabs. Also assemble the side radio by gluing the tabs and then glue on the antenna.

3 Glue the side radio to the right side of the head. Glue the headlamp and helmet to the face. Insert the neck tube into the hole at the base of the head so that it fits snugly but can still move freely.

4 Cut, score, and fold the pieces for the torso and backpack and also the supporting pivot bars. Cut out all the interior shapes marked with an "x."

* Note: If you find the pivot bars are too fiddly to make, you can try covering a stick of balsa wood with some card and cutting it to size.

5 Assemble the torso pieces, gluing the tabs, and glue them together. Make sure that the red lines on the front are aligned and glue the backpack.

6

Cut, score, and fold the pieces for the shoulders and arms. Also cut out all the interior shapes marked with an "x."

9

Carefully cut out the piece for the rotor wheel and the supporting pivot bar. Assemble the rotor wheel.

7

Assemble the pieces for the arms by gluing the tabs.

10

Insert a pivot bar onto the side of the upper arm. Glue the other end to the rotor wheel. Repeat steps 8-10 for the other arm.

8

Glue the hand to the forearm. Attach the forearm to the gray elbow piece using a short pivot bar. Next, attach the top of the elbow piece to the upper arm using a short pivot bar. Finally, attach the upper arm to the shoulder piece using a short pivot bar. Each time, glue two of the small circles to either end of the pivot bars when in place.

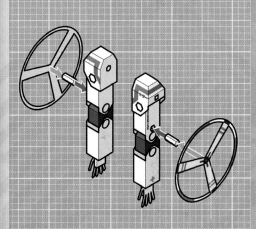

11

Cut, score, and fold the leg and foot pieces and the supporting pivot bars.

12

Assemble the pieces for the legs by gluing the tabs.

13

Glue the side attachment to to the lower leg piece. Attach the gray knee piece to the lower and upper legs using the short pivot bars, gluing the small circle pieces to the ends of the pivot bars when in place. Then glue the yellow and gray kneecap to the top of the lower leg and knee, with the yellow strip facing upwards. Assemble the foot and attach to assembled legs using short pivot bars. Repeat for the other leg.

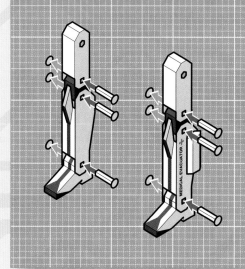

14

Attach arms to shoulders using short pivot bars and attach legs to torso using long pivot bar, gluing this closed with the small circle cap when in place.

15

Finally, attach the head to the torso, inserting the neck into the torso slot.

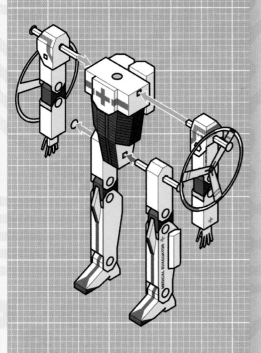

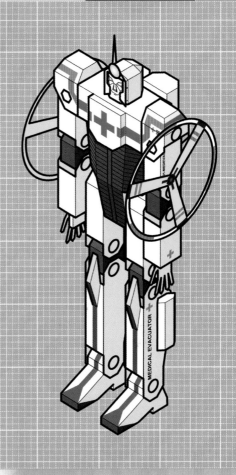

DOGBOT

FIREPOWER

STRENGTH

MANEUVERABILITY

ARMOR

INTELLIGENCE

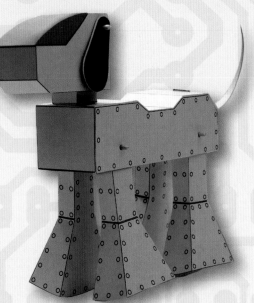

Dogbot is highly intelligent and well trained. Able to negotiate slopes with ease, Dogbot has good mobility. A wagging tail and swinging ears promote a friendly and affectionate exterior. Don't be fooled though, Dogbot's superior sense of smell makes this bot a skilled tracker, able to sniff out rivals from a hundred miles away. A thick plated metal armor means he can withstand bullets, knives, explosions, and all manner of armed offenses.

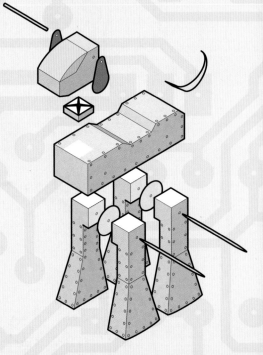

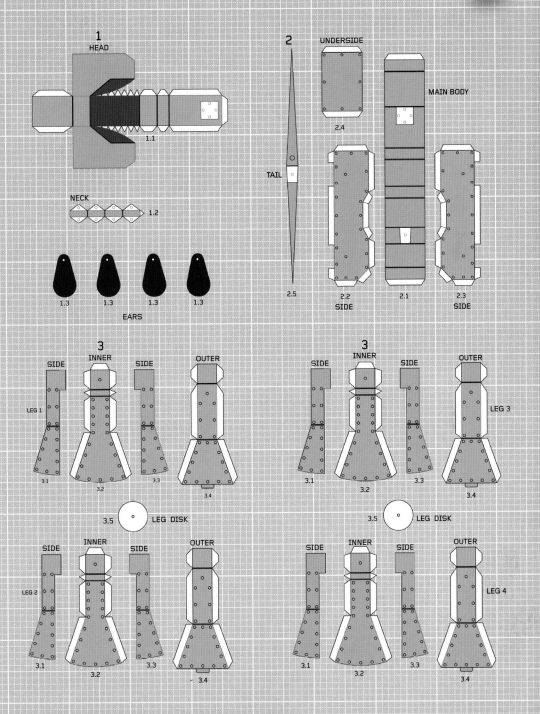

1
HEAD

1.1

NECK
1.2

EARS
1.3 1.3 1.3 1.3

2

UNDERSIDE
2.4

MAIN BODY

TAIL

2.5

2.2
SIDE

2.1

2.3
SIDE

3

SIDE INNER SIDE OUTER

LEG 1

3.1 3.2 3.3 3.4

3.5 LEG DISK

3

SIDE INNER SIDE OUTER

LEG 3

3.1 3.2 3.3 3.4

3.5 LEG DISK

SIDE INNER SIDE OUTER

LEG 2

3.1 3.2 3.3 3.4

SIDE INNER SIDE OUTER

LEG 4

3.1 3.2 3.3 3.4

1
Cut out all the shapes and punch out the marked holes by placing the paper onto a soft surface (such as carpet) and using a pen or pencil.

2
Score along the lines, fold and assemble the head, gluing the tabs. Then score along the lines, fold and assemble the neck marked 1.2, and glue it to the head marked 1.1.

3
Take a toothpick cut to 1.2 inches (3 cm), slide it through the holes on either side of the head and glue the ears. Slide them onto the toothpick ends.

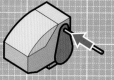

4
Score along the lines, fold, and assemble the body parts to make the main body, gluing the tabs.

5
Score and fold the tail marked 2.5. Then curl it around something cylindrical, like a pen, and glue the end tab to the body.

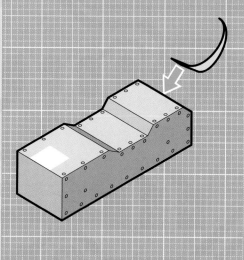

6

Score, fold, and assemble the pieces that make the leg (3), and glue the tabs. Repeat for the other legs.

7

Slide the legs in pairs onto toothpicks, with the leg disk (3.5) in between, and slide the toothpicks into the body.

8

Place Dogbot onto a rough surface, sloped at an angle of between 10 and 15 degrees—and watch him go walking! You can use books or other materials to prop up your slope.

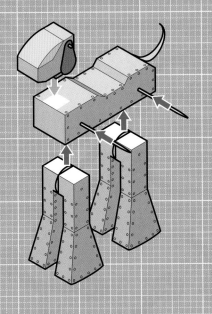

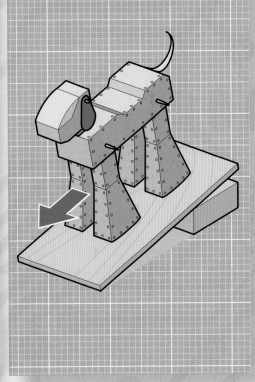

TANKBOT

FIREPOWER

STRENGTH

MANEUVERABILITY

ARMOR

INTELLIGENCE

Tankbot is the ultimate battle machine. Equipped
with missile launchers, rotating miniguns, movable
cannons, and clenched fists for battering rams,
this is the robot with the most firepower in
its arsenal. Tankbot's fortified wheelbase
means that it can move on virtually every
type of terrain and heavy-duty
steel armor protects the bot
from anti-tank attacks. Not known
for intelligence though, a faulty circuit
or electrical failure can cause Tankbot's aim to
malfunction, shooting at anything that moves.

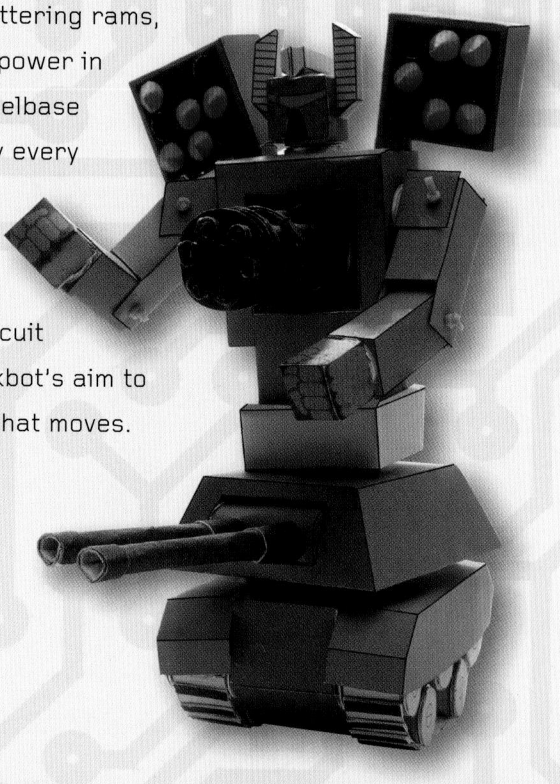

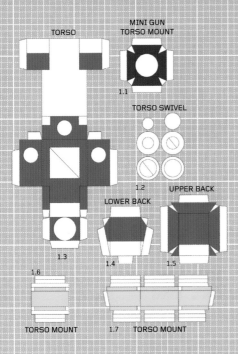

TORSO

MINI GUN
TORSO MOUNT

1.1

TORSO SWIVEL

1.2

LOWER BACK

UPPER BACK

1.3

1.4

1.5

1.6

TORSO MOUNT

1.7 TORSO MOUNT

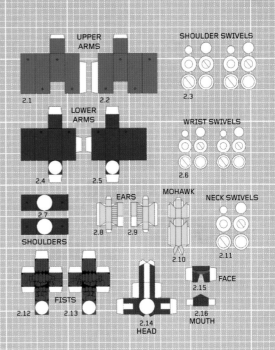

UPPER ARMS

2.1   2.2

SHOULDER SWIVELS

2.3

LOWER ARMS

2.4   2.5

WRIST SWIVELS

2.6

2.7

SHOULDERS

EARS

2.8   2.9

MOHAWK

2.10

NECK SWIVELS

2.11

FISTS

2.12   2.13

HEAD

2.14

FACE

2.15

2.16
MOUTH

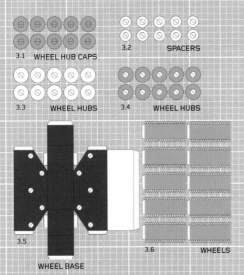

3.1 WHEEL HUB CAPS

3.2   SPACERS

3.3   WHEEL HUBS

3.4   WHEEL HUBS

3.5

WHEEL BASE

3.6   WHEELS

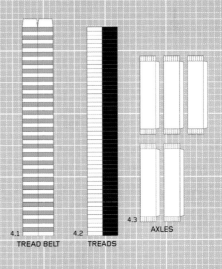

4.1
TREAD BELT

4.2
TREADS

4.3

AXLES

CANNON MOUNT

WHEELBASE TOP SWIVEL

5.1

MISSILE
LAUNCHERS

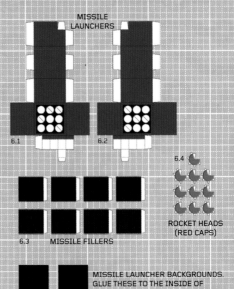

6.1

6.2

6.4

ROCKET HEADS
(RED CAPS)

CANNONS

5.3

CANNON ENDS

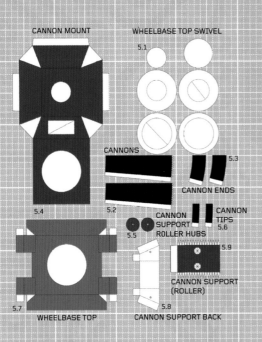

5.4

5.2

CANNON
SUPPORT
ROLLER HUBS

CANNON
TIPS
5.6

5.5

5.9

CANNON SUPPORT
(ROLLER)

6.3   MISSILE FILLERS

5.7

WHEELBASE TOP

5.8

CANNON SUPPORT BACK

MISSILE LAUNCHER BACKGROUNDS.
GLUE THESE TO THE INSIDE OF
MISSILE LAUNCHER

6.5

MINIGUNS

7.3

7.1

7.2

MIDDLE GUN BARREL

MIDDLE SUPPORT
RING STRIP

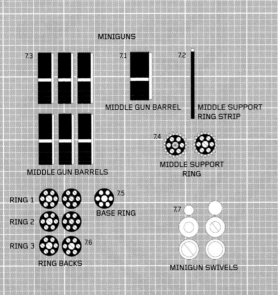

7.4

MIDDLE SUPPORT
RING

MIDDLE GUN BARRELS

RING 1

7.5

BASE RING

RING 2

7.7

RING 3

7.6

RING BACKS

MINIGUN SWIVELS

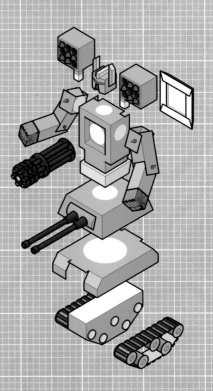

1 Cut out the disk pieces for the swivels. These will act as the main joints for Tankbot, to be added as you assemble the main parts. All the swivels follow the same construction.

2 Glue smallest circle to the middle of the large circle marked with a corresponding outline for the smaller circle.

Cut out the centers of both the rings. This should be marked with a line across the area to be cut out.

Glue the two rings together, with the larger ring on top.

Place, but do not glue, the rings onto the large circle so that the small circle shows through the hole in the bottom ring. Then glue the medium-sized circle to the smallest circle only.

Attach pivots by gluing only the upper ring to the remaining large circle base. Allow glue to dry and then twist to ensure that the circle base spins.

3 Assemble the face and mouth pieces, gluing the tabs, and attach to the head. Glue the ears and mohawk to the head.

4 Cut out, score, and fold the pieces for the arms. Assemble the upper arm, lower arm, and fist, gluing the tabs.

5 Thread the shoulder, upper arm, and lower arm together with rubber bands. Attach fist to lower arms using the wrist swivel marked 2.6. Repeat for the second arm.

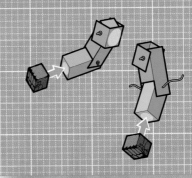

6 Cut out, score, and fold the torso pieces, using valley folds for the minigun torso mount.

7 Assemble main torso piece, gluing upper and lower backs to the torso.

8 Cut, score, and fold the missile launchers, cutting out the interior circles marked with a line across. Glue the missile launcher backgrounds marked 6.5 to the inside of the third fold segment of the missile launcher piece 6.1 and 6.2. The backgrounds should cover the white area that will be seen through the holes in the missile launcher. Glue torso shut.

9 Coil the fillers marked 6.3 into tubes so that the inside is black, glue tabs closed, and slot into holes of 6.1 and 6.2. Glue red caps to white circles.

10 Assemble minigun. Cut out the holes in the rings and glue rings marked 7.6 to ring backs also marked 7.6. Assemble middle support ring marked 7.4 gluing the ring strip (7.2) to the tabs around the rings, joining the two. Coil barrels 7.1 and 7.3 and slide through the rings. Glue to ring base marked 7.5.

11 Add minigun, arms, and head with swivels to torso.

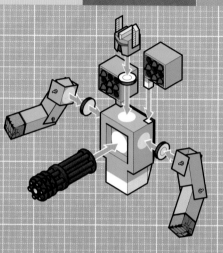

12 Cut, score, and fold the pieces for the wheels, treads, and wheelbase. Also cut out the interior shapes marked with a line across the center. Cut out the black and white strips of 4.2. Assemble wheelbase, gluing the tabs.

13 Coil the wheels. On one side of the wheel, glue the white wheel hubs marked 3.3. On the other side, glue the gray hubs marked 3.4. The side with the white hubs will go on the inside of the wheel facing the wheel base. Cut the tips of the axles into strips so they are like tassels. Slot axles into wheelbase, then slide the spacers (3.2) and wheels onto axles. Fold the tassel-like axle tips over wheel hubs (3.3 and 3.4) so they fan out. Now glue the wheel hubcaps marked 3.1 to the outside of the wheel, gluing the wheel shut.

14

Assemble treads by first gluing white strips to the tread belt (4.1) and then glue the black strips to the white strips.

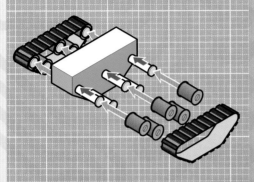

15

Cut out, score, and fold the pieces for the cannons and the cannon supports.

16

Assemble cannons, gluing the tabs. Attach 5.2, 5.3, and 5.6 to form the cannons. Thread through the cannon support (roller) and attach white back to the roller.

17

Attach all the componenents using the swivels.

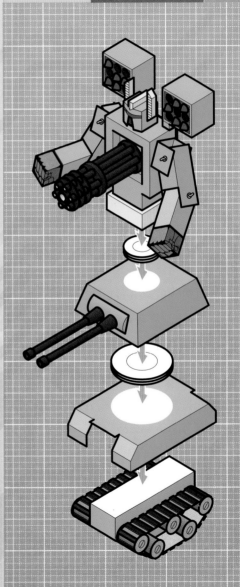

CYBERBOT

FIREPOWER

STRENGTH

MANEUVERABILITY

ARMOR

INTELLIGENCE

Cyberbot is the brains behind any operation. This robot is
a storehouse of information past, present, and future. The
large upper body communicates with parallel dimensions.
A powerful exoskeleton is protected by a stealth armor
that makes up for Cyberbot's lack of weaponry.
With articulated joints and leg haunches,
Cyberbot is highly mobile and is able
to maneuver out of sticky situations. A
homing beacon on top of the main body
serves to alert others to danger and
send out distress calls.

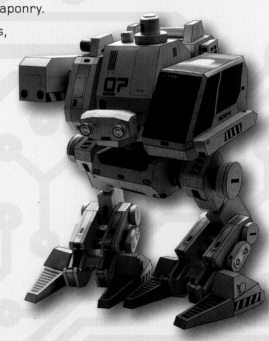

BODY COMPONENTS
(1-10, 14, 17, 19, 20, 29, 36)

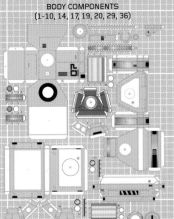

BODY COMPONENTS
(13, 18, 21, 22, 25, 28, 29, 36)

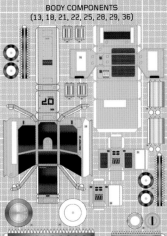

BODY COMPONENTS
(15, 16. 24, 26, 27, 30, 31, 33, 40)

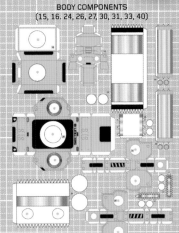

BODY COMPONENTS
(11, 32-35, 37, 39, 41)

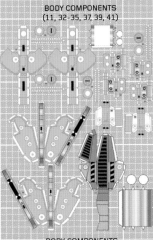

BODY COMPONENTS
(12, 23, 25, 41)

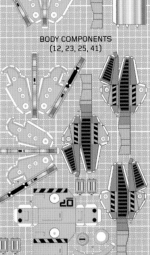

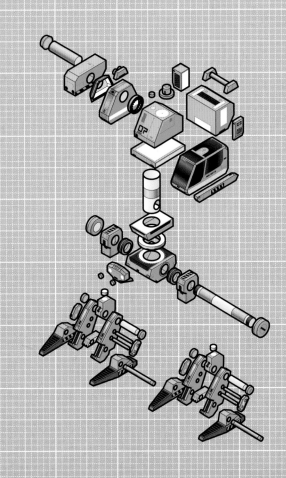

1 Cut, score, and fold the parts for the main body marked 1 and 2. Also cut out the interior shapes marked with a *.

2 Using the white tabs marked with a dot as a guide, glue and assemble parts 1 and 2. Apply glue on the large rectangles marked with a dot and glue 1 and 2 together.

3 Cut, score, and fold the parts for the main body marked 13, 14, 15, 16, and 17, also cutting out the interior shapes marked with a *.

4 Assemble parts 13, 14, and 15, by gluing the tabs, to complete half of the upper body. Attach the assembled head, piece 16, and the eye pieces marked 17. (Part 15 attaches to piece 2.)

5 Carefully cut out part 18, 19, 20, 21, and 22, and the interior shapes marked with a *.

6 Assemble these pieces by gluing the tabs and glue 21 the left side of 18. Glue 22 to the right side of 18. Glue one piece of part 19 to the top of 18 on one side, then glue part 20 to this piece. Finally glue the second part of 19 to the top of 18 and then glue this to 20.

7 Carefully cut out part 3, cutting along the teeth. Score and then curl it around something cylindrical, like a marker pen or your finger.

8

Glue it together and attach it to the large black-rimmed white circle on part 1.

9

Carefully cut out all the pieces marked 7, 8, and 9.

10

Assemble piece 7 by curling the strip around something cylindrical, and gluing the yellow disk on top. Glue the assembled piece 7 to the large white circle with a red dot on part 1. Then glue the assembled pieces of part 8 to part 7. Attach assembled part 9 to the small circle marked with a dot on part 1.

11

Cut, score, and fold the pieces numbered 4, 5, 6, 10, 11, 12, and 23 ,and assemble by gluing the tabs. Also cut out the interior shapes marked with a *.

12

Slide part 11 through the open holes in parts 23, 10, and 4. Glue part 12 to 23. Assemble and glue parts 5 and 6 to part 4 to complete the left-hand side of the upper body.

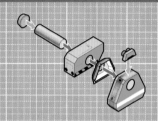

13

Cut, score, and fold the pieces for parts 24, 25, 26, 27, and 28. Also cut out the interior shapes marked with a *.

14

Assemble these pieces gluing the tabs, and coil 24 and 27 into long cylinders, gluing the white disks to the ends. Assemble 25 and then glue this to the top of 26, keeping the holes aligned. Slide 24 through 25 and 26, making sure that only the gray strip is visible. Slide 27 through the two side holes in 26 so that the two gray strips are visible. Then slide the two pieces makred 28 on to either end of 27.

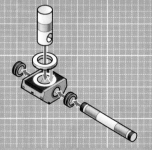

15

To assemble the legs, begin by cutting out all the pieces marked 29–41. Note that there should be two sets of each piece, one for either side. Also cut out the interior shapes marked with a *. Score and fold these.

16

Assemble these, gluing the tabs, and then glue part 30 to 32. Assemble parts 33, 34, and 35, and then slide 33 through the holes in 35, 32, and the second 35 piece. Cover 33 with the hubs marked 34. Also slide the two 36 bars through 35 and glue 37 to the ends on either side.

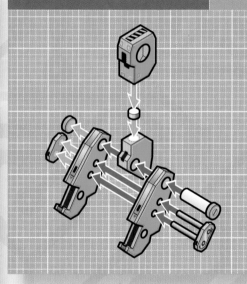

17

Assemble pieces 38, 39, 40, and 41. Slide the bar marked 40 through one of the toe pieces marked 41, one of the leg pieces marked 35, and the middle piece 39. Then slide the bar through the other 35 and slot the other toe piece 41 onto the end of the leg to complete the foot. Carefully glue the tubes marked 38 to the bottom grooves of part 35, with two on either side. (Note: Pieces 38 are optional and not shown in diagram.)

19

Finally, attach the legs to the main body by slotting part 27 through the holes in part 30. Assemble the joint hubs with the part marked 29 and attach these to the end of 27 to complete the robot.

18

Repeat this process to complete the second leg.

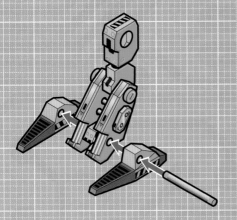

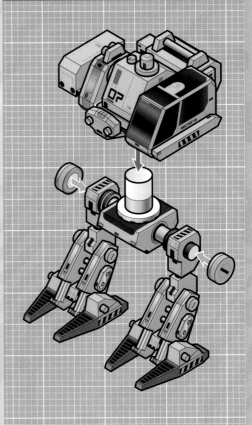

BOLOBOT

FIREPOWER

STRENGTH

MANEUVERABILITY

ARMOR

INTELLIGENCE

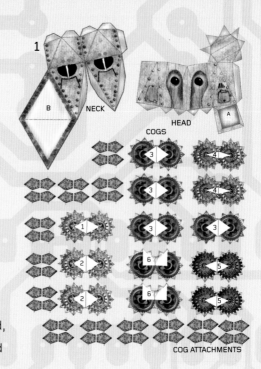

Bolobot is an extra-terrestrial android, most useful for space explorations and asteroid studies. Although not armed with any weapons, Bolo has the unique ability to communicate in all known space and earthly languages. The articulated joints not only provide him with mobility but are Bolo's vocal tools—each different combination of arm, neck, and leg movements results in a different language. His communication skills and powers of negotiation are a diplomatic blessing.

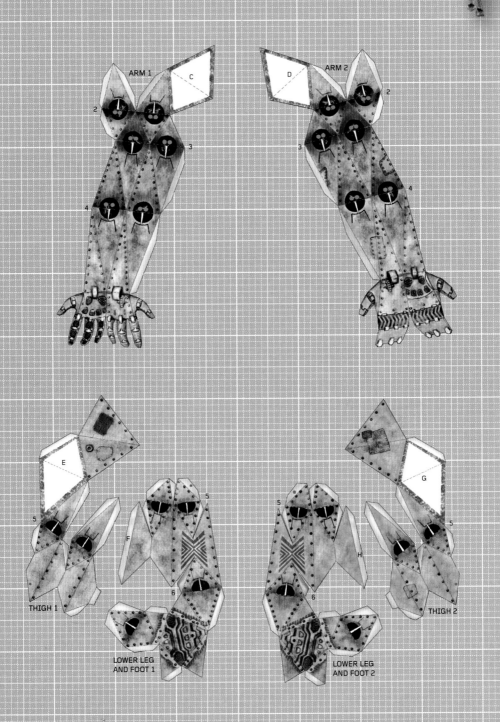

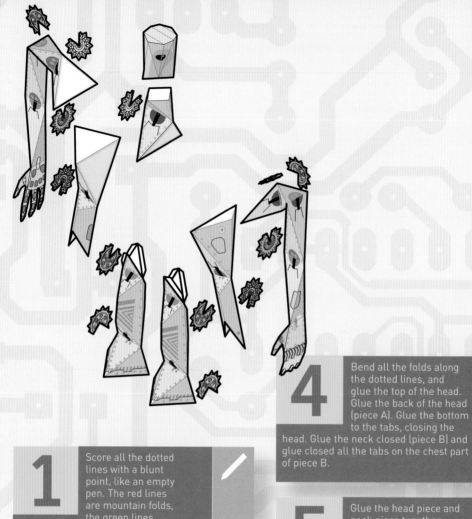

4

Bend all the folds along the dotted lines, and glue the top of the head. Glue the back of the head (piece A). Glue the bottom to the tabs, closing the head. Glue the neck closed (piece B) and glue closed all the tabs on the chest part of piece B.

1

Score all the dotted lines with a blunt point, like an empty pen. The red lines are mountain folds, the green lines valley folds.

2

Cut out all the cog attachments with a modeling knife or scissors before separating the pieces. Also cut out the small white rectangle that goes down to the tab on the body parts, where the cogs will fit in later.

3

Cut out the pieces following the black outlines.

5

Glue the head piece and neck piece together (pieces A to B).

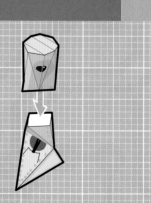

6

Assemble the arm pieces (C and D), gluing the tabs.

7

Assemble and glue the leg and thigh pieces (parts G and H), gluing the tabs, and glue together at the red dot.

8

Repeat for the other leg (parts E and F).

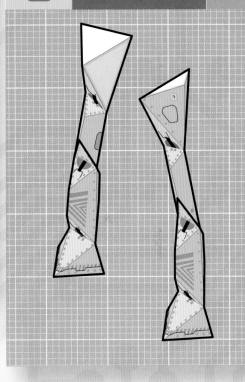

9

Join the legs, the arms, and the head with glue to assemble the body.

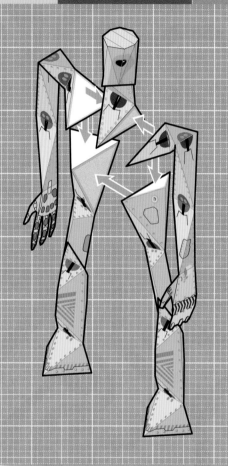

10

To make the cogs, cut a rectangle around them, fold them in half along the dotted line and glue together. Then cut the teeth outline with scissors and cut out the white triangle. Keep a note of the number, as each cog has a different angle.

11

Place the cog in the corresponding slot, making sure the center of the cog is aligned with the green dots.

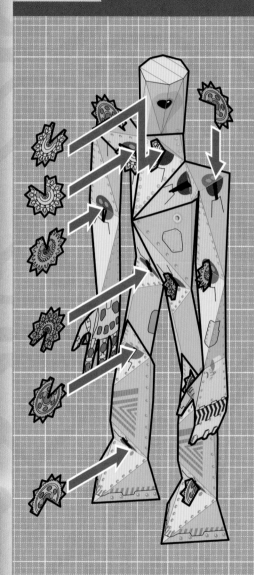

12 Bend all the cog attachments, gluing them against the cog and the body, covering the green dots. Be careful that you do not glue the cog to the body otherwise your Bolo will not be able to speak!

The cog attachments.

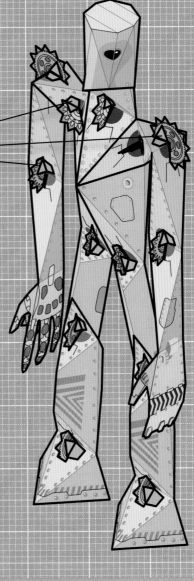

BLAZEFIGHTER

FIREPOWER

STRENGTH

MANEUVERABILITY

ARMOR

INTELLIGENCE

Blazefighter is the ultimate firefighting weapon. The fire-resistant armor can withstand heat up to 3000°F without any damage. Equipped with a backpack that stores over 2000 gallons of water, this highly intelligent and responsive robot can single-handedly tend to most fire emergencies. The water thrust from the arm hose can penetrate flames from as far as three miles away. The left arm is a cartridge-operated carbon-dioxide extinguisher designed to suppress chemical fires. Blazefighter's fireproof, all-terrain track wheels enable him to access sites that are isolated and difficult for ordinary firefighters to reach.

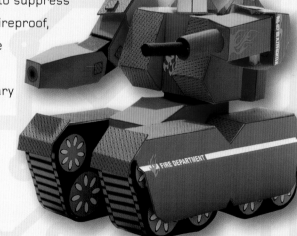

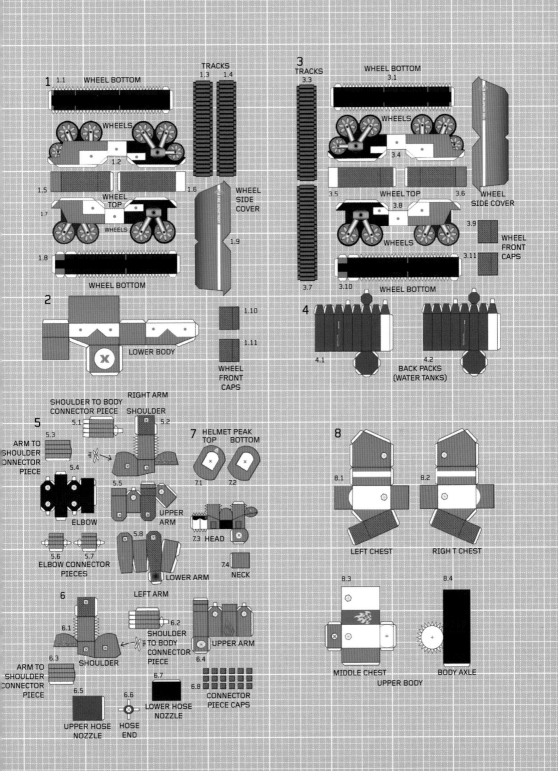

1 1.1 WHEEL BOTTOM

TRACKS
1.3 1.4

1.5 1.6

WHEEL TOP

1.2

WHEELS

1.7

WHEELS

1.8

WHEEL BOTTOM

WHEEL SIDE COVER
1.9

3 TRACKS
3.3

WHEEL BOTTOM
3.1

WHEELS

3.4

3.5 WHEEL TOP 3.6

3.8

WHEELS

WHEEL SIDE COVER

3.9

WHEEL FRONT CAPS

3.11

3.7 3.10 WHEEL BOTTOM

2

LOWER BODY

1.10

1.11

WHEEL FRONT CAPS

4

4.1 4.2 BACK PACKS (WATER TANKS)

5

SHOULDER TO BODY CONNECTOR PIECE

5.1

RIGHT ARM

SHOULDER 5.2

5.3

ARM TO SHOULDER CONNECTOR PIECE

5.4

5.5

UPPER ARM

ELBOW

5.6 5.7

ELBOW CONNECTOR PIECES

5.8

LOWER ARM

7 HELMET PEAK
TOP BOTTOM

7.1 7.2

7.3 HEAD

7.4 NECK

8

8.1 8.2

LEFT CHEST RIGHT T CHEST

8.3 8.4

MIDDLE CHEST BODY AXLE

UPPER BODY

6

6.1

LEFT ARM

6.2

SHOULDER TO BODY CONNECTOR PIECE

UPPER ARM

6.4

6.3 SHOULDER

ARM TO SHOULDER CONNECTOR PIECE

6.7

6.8 CONNECTOR PIECE CAPS

6.5

6.6

LOWER HOSE NOZZLE

UPPER HOSE NOZZLE

HOSE END

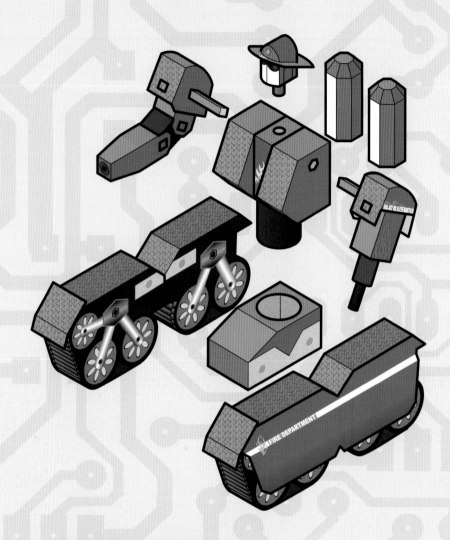

1 Cut out all the pieces and the interior holes marked with a red "x." Then cut through just the diagonal red lines in certain holes to make small tabs and push these tabs through with a suitable tool (such as a pen or a pencil).

2 Score along the fold lines, and fold and assemble the wheel and track units, gluing the tabs. Glue together.

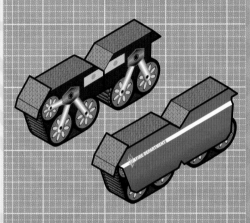

3 Assemble the lower body part marked 2, gluing the tabs. Glue assembled wheel units to lower body part.

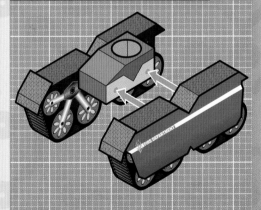

4 Score along the lines, fold and assemble all three chest parts (8.1–8.3) that make up the upper body, gluing the tabs. Then cut out the black main body axle and curl it around a pen, or something cylindrical.

5 Glue the right chest piece and the left chest to the middle chest piece. And glue the main body axle to the bottom of the middle piece.

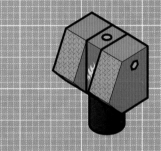

6 Cut, score, fold, and assemble the backpacks marked 4.1 and 4.2, gluing the tabs. Glue them to the back of the upper body on 8.1 and 8.2.

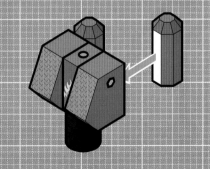

7 Join the upper body and the lower body by sliding the main body axle into the hole in the lower body part (2). Do not glue, as this will prevent it from rotating.

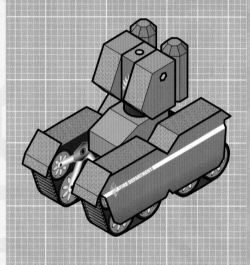

8 Assemble all the pieces for the left arm, gluing their tabs, and connect them together using the connector pieces, and sliding them through the cut out holes.

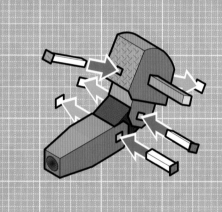

9 Repeat for the right arm.

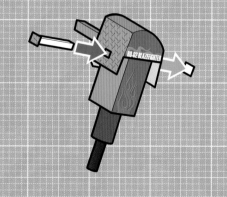

10
Slot the arms into the body using the connector pieces.

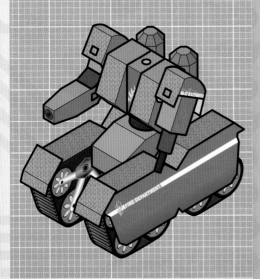

12
Slot the neck into the middle chest piece. Do not glue if you want it to rotate.

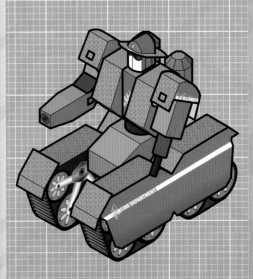

11
Assemble the head pieces, gluing the tabs, and gluing on the helmet. Coil the neck, glue the tab, and glue to the head.

CONSTRUCTOR

FIREPOWER

STRENGTH

MANEUVERABILITY

ARMOR

INTELLIGENCE

1

SEAT FRAME (GLUE TAB TO BACK OF DOTS ON LOWER CHAMBER)

LOWER FOOT CHAMBER (GLUE FOOT PEDALS TO MARKS)

BELTS
1.1

BUCKLES
1.2   1.3

COCKPIT SEAT

1.4
STRAPS

1.5

1.6

1.7
CONTROL PANEL

1.8
STEERING FRONT

1.9
STEERING BACK

1.10
RIGHT PANEL

LEFT PANEL
1.11

1.12

1.13
WINDOW PANE DIMENSIONS

X   X   X

GLUE
CONTROL
PANEL HERE
INNER CHAMBER

1.14
FOOT PEDALS

Constructor does exactly what it says on the tin. This highly sophisticated and intelligent robot was designed to construct things and is architect and builder all in one. Opposed to violence and destruction, Constructor has no weapons, but uses its powerful, sturdy, and extendable body to intimidate attackers. The strong Halogen-powered flashlights mean that it can work day or night. The cockpit area is the powerhouse of all operations from where this robot is able to outwit its opponents, lay out and execute plans for complicated building structures, and of course, chill out and listen to some music.

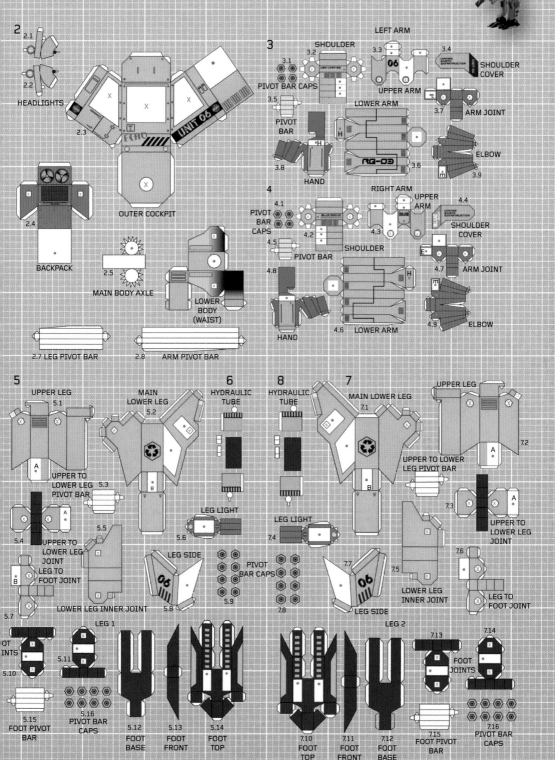

2

2.1
2.2

HEADLIGHTS

2.3 UNIT 06

OUTER COCKPIT

2.4

BACKPACK

2.5 MAIN BODY AXLE

LOWER BODY (WAIST)

2.7 LEG PIVOT BAR

2.8 ARM PIVOT BAR

3 LEFT ARM

SHOULDER
3.2
3.1
PIVOT BAR CAPS

3.3
3.4 SHOULDER COVER
UPPER ARM 06

3.5
PIVOT BAR
LOWER ARM
3.7 ARM JOINT

3.8
HAND
H
RG-03
3.6
ELBOW
3.9

4 RIGHT ARM
4.1
PIVOT BAR CAPS
UPPER ARM
4.4 SHOULDER COVER
BLUE GROUP
4.2
4.3
4.5
PIVOT BAR
SHOULDER
4.7 ARM JOINT
E
4.8
H
HAND
4.6 LOWER ARM
4.9 ELBOW

5
UPPER LEG
5.1
A
UPPER TO LOWER LEG 5.3 PIVOT BAR

MAIN LOWER LEG
5.2

6
HYDRAULIC TUBE

8
HYDRAULIC TUBE

7
MAIN LOWER LEG
7.1

UPPER LEG
7.2

UPPER TO LOWER LEG PIVOT BAR

5.4
UPPER TO LOWER LEG JOINT
LEG TO FOOT JOINT
B
5.5
LEG SIDE 06
LOWER LEG INNER JOINT 5.8

LEG LIGHT
5.6
PIVOT BAR CAPS
5.9

LEG LIGHT
7.4

7.3
UPPER TO LOWER LEG JOINT
A

7.5
LOWER LEG INNER JOINT
7.7
7.8
LEG SIDE 06

7.6
LEG TO FOOT JOINT

LEG 1
OT INTS
5.10
5.11
5.15 FOOT PIVOT BAR
5.16 PIVOT BAR CAPS
5.12 FOOT BASE
5.13 FOOT FRONT
5.14 FOOT TOP

LEG 2
7.13
7.14
FOOT JOINTS
7.10 FOOT TOP
7.11 FOOT FRONT
7.12 FOOT BASE
7.15 FOOT PIVOT BAR
7.16 PIVOT BAR CAPS

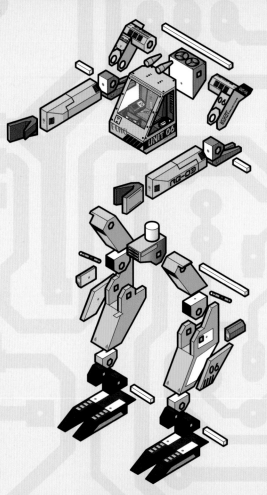

3 Glue the gray part of the cockpit chamber (1.12) to the outer body (2.3). Glue and assemble the outer body of the cockpit, gluing the tabs and using transparent plastic as the front glass, leaving the side windows empty.

4 Assemble the backpack and top headlights, gluing the tabs, and glue to the cockpit.

5 Cut, score, and fold the arm pivot bar marked 2.8, and assemble gluing the tabs.

* Note: If you find the pivot bars are too fiddly to make, you can try covering a stick of balsa wood with some card paper and cutting it to size.

6 Slide the pivot bars through the back attachment for the shoulders.

1 Cut, score, and fold the pieces marked 1 and 2 for the cockpit inner chamber and the outer cockpit. Also cut out the interior shapes marked with an "x."

2 Carefully assemble the inner chamber and cockpit, gluing the panel pieces, steering wheel, pedals, and right and left panels (1.1–1.11) to the inner cockpit chamber (1.12).

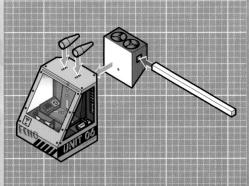

7
Cut, score, and fold the pieces for the arms marked 3 and 4. Also cut out the interior shapes marked with an "x."

8
Assemble the main arm pieces, gluing the tabs.

9
To make the arm, slide the pivot bars for the arm joint marked 3.7/4.7 into the hexagonal hole on the arm joint piece. Glue the pivot bar in place and attach the lower arm and hand to the arm joint. Finally, attach the shoulder to the upper arm and slide on to shoulder pivot bar. Cover the axle joints with the shoulder cover.

10
Repeat this step for the other arm.

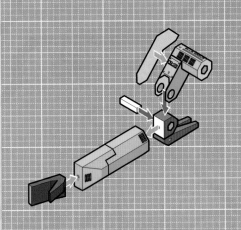

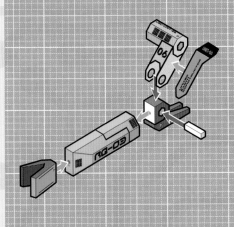

11 Cut, score, and fold the pieces for the lower body. Also cut out the interior shapes marked with an "x."

12 Coil the white body axle marked 2.5 round comething cylindrical, and glue using the tabs. Assemble the pivot bar and the waist marked 2.8.

13 Assemble the lower body by sliding the pivot bar for the legs (2.7) through the holes in the waist piece, and sliding the body axle through the hole in the top.

14 Cut, score, and fold the pieces for the legs and feet, cutting out any interior holes marked with an "x."

15 Assemble the individual pieces by gluing their tabs.

16 Assemble the feet and legs by sliding the pivot bars into the hexagonal holes. Glue pivot bars in place and cover with the caps.

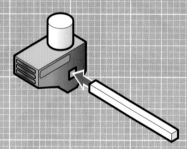

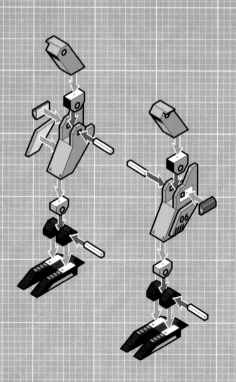

17

Cut, score, and fold the pieces for the hydraulic suspension, marked 6 and 8.

18

Coil the pieces around something cylindrical, and glue the tabs. Each set should have three pieces; one gray tube, and two yellow tubes.

19

The yellow tubes should be slightly wider than the gray tubes. Slide the yellow tubes onto the ends of the gray tube so that they fit snugly on either end. Do not glue these.

20

Next, glue the yellow tubes to the upper leg and knee parts, using the separate white rectangle tabs.

21

To complete, attach legs to the pivot bars on the lower body part and slide the cockpit onto the waist axle.

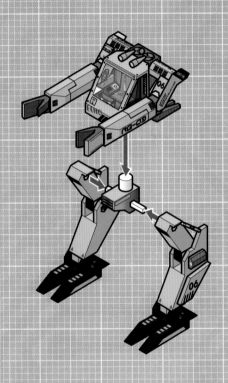

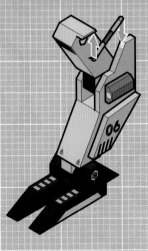

DESTRUCTOR

FIREPOWER

STRENGTH

MANEUVERABILITY

ARMOR

INTELLIGENCE

Destructor is Constructor's arch nemesis. Although Destructor has no firing weapons, he can wreck towering structures with his iron-bending claws and reduce buildings to rubble simply by driving into them with his super-strength aligned crystal-steel armor. The plow component helps Destructor remove debris and clear the path for attack. Although mobile, Destructor has limited maneuverability but the highly charged laser and X-ray lens on the upper body help the robot identify its targets' weakest points and destroy it with minimal effort.

BODY COMPONENTS
(1-12)

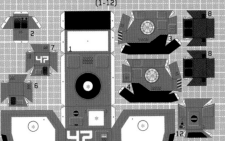

BASE COMPONENTS
(13-20)

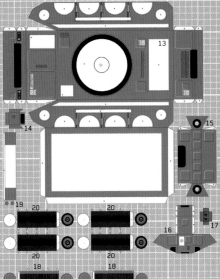

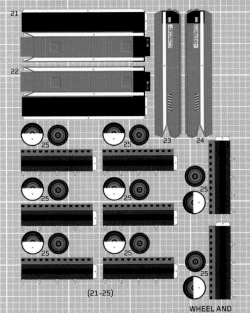

(21-25)

WHEEL AND WHEELBASE COMPONENTS

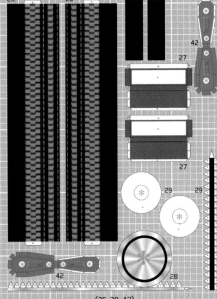

(26-29, 42)

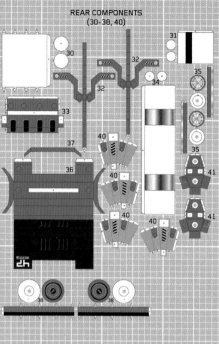

REAR COMPONENTS
(30-38, 40)

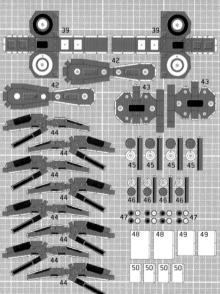

CLAW COMPONENTS
(39, 42-50)

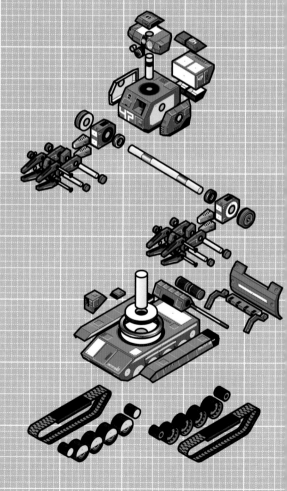

1 Cut, score, and fold the pieces marked 1 and 3–8 for the top body, cockpit, and cabin. Also cut out the interior areas marked with a *.

4 Cut, score, and fold the pieces marked 9–12 for the viewing cabin. Also cut out the interior areas marked with a *.

2 Assemble pieces 1 and 3–8, gluing the tabs. Cut out piece 2 and fold inward, using valley folds.

5 Assemble pieces 9–12, gluing the tabs. Coil 10 and 11 round something cylindrical and glue them closed using the tabs.

3 Glue part 2 in the hollow space at the front of part 1. Now glue parts 3 and 4 to either sides of part 1, keeping the holes aligned. Glue part 8 under part 5 and glue 6 and 7 to the top. Now glue part 5 to the rear of part 1.

6 Glue part 11 to the small circle and part 10 to the large circle marked on part 9. Then glue part 12 to the top of part 9.

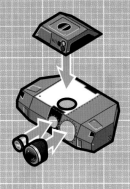

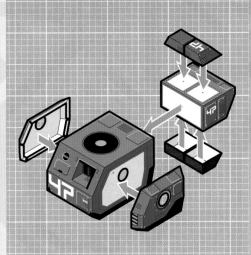

7 Cut, score, and fold the pieces marked 13–19 for the main body of Destructor. Also cut out the interior areas marked with a *.

8 Assemble pieces 13–19, gluing the tabs.

9 Glue part 14 to the top of 13 on the right-hand side. Glue part 17 to part 16 and then glue this on the front left-hand side of part 13. Glue part 18 to part 15 and slide 19 through the holes in part 15. Now glue 15 to the rear of part 13.

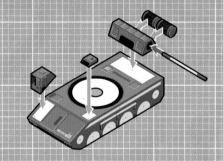

10 Cut, score, and fold the pieces marked 20–27 for the wheels and treads. Also cut out the interior areas marked with a *.

11 First assemble the wheels with pieces 20 and 25. Coil the strips around something cylindrical and glue closed with their main tab. Glue the white (or half white) wheel hub to one end of the tube. Slide and glue the colored hub into the tube. Each set of wheels should have four large wheels and two small wheels.

12 Glue the wheels to the main body part 13. Also glue part 27 to the underside of the tire tread strip marked 26. Then wind the strip around the wheels and glue it shut to form a tread loop.

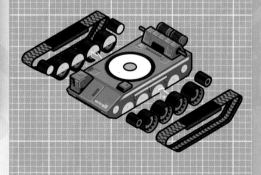

13

Next glue part 21 to the left side above the wheels and glue 22 to the right side. Glue part 23 to part 22 and glue part 24 to part 21.

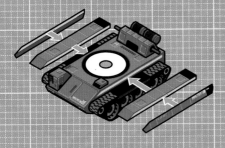

14

Cut, score, and fold the pieces marked 28–31 for the pivots. Also cut out the interior areas marked with a *.

15

Coil the pieces marked 30 and 31 round something cylindrical and assemble, gluing the tabs.

16

Slot the tube marked 30 into the holes in 28 and 29 and then into the main body (part 13). Next slot the tube marked 31 into the top of the top body piece marked 5 and then slot 5 onto the tube marked 30 so that it now rests snugly on the main body. Finally, slot the viewing cabin body marked 9 onto the tube marked 31.

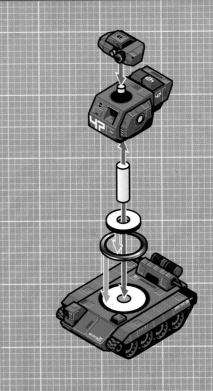

17

Cut, score, and fold the pieces marked 32–37 for the plow, coiling where necessary as before. Also cut out the interior areas marked with a *.

18

Assemble these pieces, gluing the tabs.

19

Slide the tube marked 34 through the main body and the holes on parts 3 and 4. Glue 37 to 36 to form the main plow. Next, glue the two arms marked 32 to the back of 36. Also glue the rear piece marked 33 to the back of 36. Place this at the rear of the body and slide the two arms 32 onto the tube marked 19.

20

Cut, score, and fold the pieces marked 38–50, coiling where necessary, for the arms and claws. Also cut out the interior areas marked with a *.

21

Assemble the pieces, gluing the tabs.

22

Glue part 40 to 39 and 41. Slide the tube 48 through parts 41 and 42 and then cover with the hub 45. Then slide tube 49 through parts 42 and 43 and cover the tube with hub 46. Next slide both the tubes marked 50 through the top and bottom of the claws marked 44 and the part 43. Cover the tube 50 with the hub marked 47. Attach the ring marked 35 to one end of the piece marked 39, keeping the holes aligned. Repeat for the other claw.

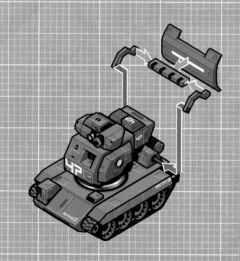

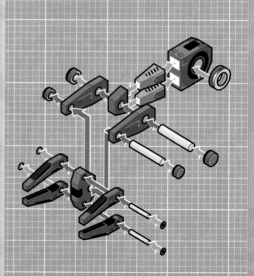

23

Finally, slide this onto one side of the piece marked 34 and then cover the end with the hub piece marked 38. Repeat for the second arm and claw.

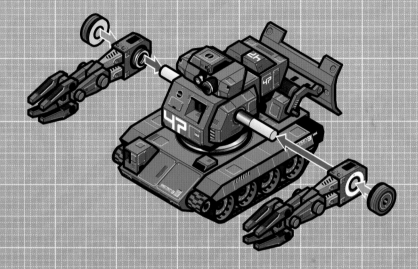

SPIDERBOT

FIREPOWER

STRENGTH

MANEUVERABILITY

ARMOR

INTELLIGENCE

Spiderbot is the most vicious and powerful fighting robot. The venom in each spike on its limbs and back is enough to destroy a small town. A single bite can kill in a matter of seconds and the web on its inner chest can trap and paralyze victims beyond rescue. Added to this are two rotating miniguns under the torso and bone-crushing claws on its arms. This highly mobile, extremely intelligent, supple beast is a killing machine, but is sometimes at a disadvantage: its gangly limbs are fragile and the thin exoskeleton has no armor to defend it.

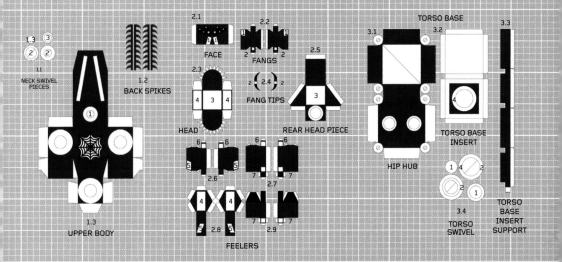

1.3 3
2 2

11
NECK SWIVEL
PIECES

1.2
BACK SPIKES

2.1
FACE

2.2
1 1
FANGS

2.5

2.3
4 3 4
HEAD

2 2.4 2
FANG TIPS

3
REAR HEAD PIECE

TORSO BASE

3.1 3.2 3.3

4

HIP HUB

TORSO BASE
INSERT

3.4
TORSO
SWIVEL

1 4 2
2 1

TORSO
BASE
INSERT
SUPPORT

6 6 6 6
5 5
2.6 2.7
7 7 7 7

4 4
2.8 5 2.9
7 7

FEELERS

1
UPPER BODY

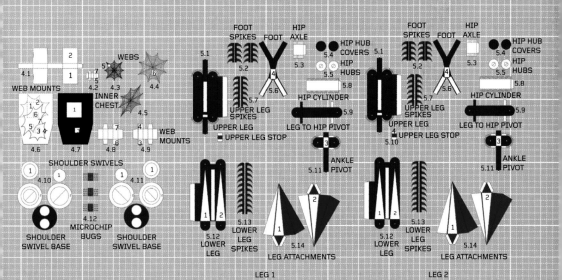

2
4.1 1
WEB MOUNTS

5 7
5
4.2

WEBS
6

4.3
INNER
CHEST

4.4

4.5

1 2
6 7
5 3 4
4.6

1
4.7

7
4.8

4
3 4.9
WEB
MOUNTS

SHOULDER SWIVELS
1 1 1
4.10 4.11

1 1

4.12
MICROCHIP
BUGS

SHOULDER
SWIVEL BASE

SHOULDER
SWIVEL BASE

FOOT
SPIKES FOOT
HIP
AXLE

5.1

5.2
4
5.3

5.6
5.4 HIP HUB
COVERS

5.5 HIP
HUBS

5.7
UPPER LEG
SPIKES
5.8
HIP CYLINDER

UPPER LEG
UPPER LEG STOP
5.9
LEG TO HIP PIVOT

3
ANKLE
5.11 PIVOT

5.12
LOWER
LEG

1 2

5.13
LOWER
LEG
SPIKES

1
2
5.14
LEG ATTACHMENTS

LEG 1

FOOT
SPIKES FOOT
HIP
AXLE

5.1

5.2
4
5.3

5.6
5.4 HIP HUB
COVERS

5.5 HIP
HUBS

5.7
UPPER LEG
SPIKES
5.8
HIP CYLINDER

UPPER LEG
4 UPPER LEG STOP
5.10
5.9
LEG TO HIP PIVOT

3
ANKLE
5.11 PIVOT

5.12
LOWER
LEG

1 2

5.13
LOWER
LEG
SPIKES

1
2
5.14
LEG ATTACHMENTS

LEG 2

82

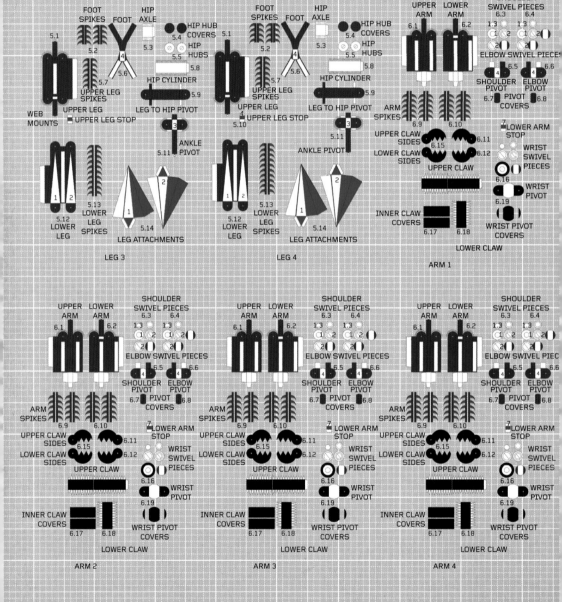

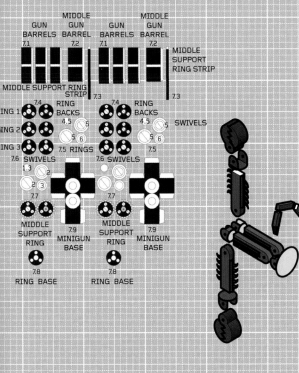

GUN
BARRELS
7.1

MIDDLE
GUN
BARREL
7.2

GUN
BARRELS
7.1

MIDDLE
GUN
BARREL
7.2

MIDDLE
SUPPORT
RING STRIP

MIDDLE SUPPORT RING
STRIP

MIDDLE
SUPPORT
RING STRIP
7.3

7.3

7.3

ING 1
7.4

RING
BACKS

7.4

RING
BACKS

ING 2
4.5
5

4.5
5

SWIVELS

ING 3
5
6

7.5
RINGS

5
6

7.5

7.6 SWIVELS

7.6 SWIVELS

1.3
2

3

7.7

7.7

MIDDLE
SUPPORT
RING

7.9
MINIGUN
BASE

MIDDLE
SUPPORT
RING

7.9
MINIGUN
BASE

7.8
RING BASE

7.8
RING BASE

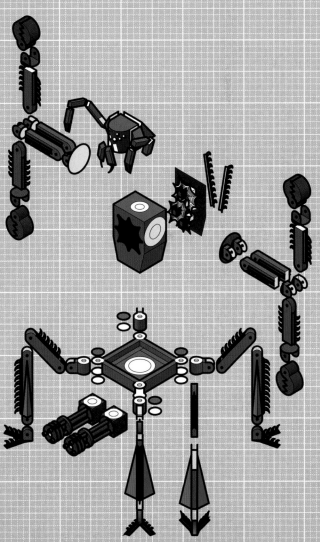

84

1 Cut out the disk pieces for the swivels. These will act as the main joints for Spiderbot, to be added as you assemble the main parts. All the swivels follow the same construction.

2 Glue smallest circle to the middle of the large circle marked with a corresponding outline for the smaller circle.

Cut out the centers of both the rings. This should be marked with a line across the area to be cut out.

Glue the two rings together, with the larger ring on top.

Place, but do not glue, the rings onto the large circle so that the small circle shows through the hole in the bottom ring. Then glue the medium-sized circle to the smallest circle only.

Attach pivots by gluing only the upper ring to the remaining large circle base. Allow glue to dry and then twist to ensure that the circle base spins.

3 Cut out and score all the pieces for the arms, arm spikes, and claws. Also cut out the interior holes marked with an "x."

4 Fold and assemble the lower arm, gluing the tabs, but leaving the circular top open. Glue the spikes to the arm.

5 Glue the pivot covers marked 6.7 and 6.8 to the inside of pieces 6.5 and 6.6. Thread a rubber band through one flap of the lower arm to the shoulder pivot marked 6.5 and then the first hole of the lower arm. Slide on a coffee stirrer or plastic straw for support.

6 Continue to thread the rubber band through the second hole of the lower arm and then glue the top shut.

7 Thread the rubber band through the second flap of the pivot. Pull the rubber band through fully, knot the edges and cut off the slack.

8 Now glue the swivel to the flat white part of the lower arm to form the wrist pivot. Assemble the triangular lower arm stop marked 6.13 and glue tab 7 to small white rectangle marked on the top of the lower arm.

17 Glue the top of the upper arms to the brown shoulder swivel base, marked with two white circles from the set numbered 4.10 and 4.11.

18 Attach the lower arms to the flat end of the upper arms. Twist all the joints to make sure they move freely, and the swivels rotate.

19 Repeat until you have four complete arms for Spiderbot.

20 Cut, score, and fold all the pieces for the legs.

21 Assemble lower and upper legs in a similar way to the arms. Attach lower leg to ankle pivot using rubber band and a coffee stick/straw.

22 Fold the foot piece in half and glue together. Glue the foot to the lower leg pivot.

23 Take the assembled upper leg and attach to lower leg using rubber bands and a coffee stirrer stick/straw for support.

24 Next, assemble the hip cylinder. For piece 5.5, cut out the circle, marked with a line across the middle. Roll the white strip marked 5.8 into a thick cylinder as wide as the hip hubs marked 5.5 and glue the side tabs to the hip hubs. Cut out 5.3, slice through the lines marked on the side (they are a bit like tassels). Roll piece 5.3 into a thin tube to form the axle and spread out the tassel-like pieces so that they fan out in a circle. You will use these axles to connect the hip cylinders to the torso (see step 46).

25

Glue the hip cylinder to the brown hip joint (5.9). Attach the hip joint to the upper leg using a rubber band and a straw.

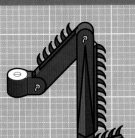

26

Repeat until you have four complete legs for Spiderbot.

27

Cut, score, and fold the pieces for the head.

28

Assemble the head pieces, gluing the tabs.

29

Glue the side and rear head pieces to the main head piece, and then glue the face to the front of the head piece.

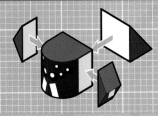

30

Cut, score, and fold the pieces for the fang tips, fangs, and the feelers.

31

Fold the fang tips, marked 2.4, in half and glue them together. Next, assemble the fangs, marked 2.2, gluing the tabs, and glue the fang tips to the ends.

32

Assemble the feelers, using pieces 2.6, 2.7, 2.8, and 2.9, gluing the tabs. Glue 2.6, 2.7, and 2.9 together. Then glue 2.9 to 2.8, and 2.8 to the side of the head. Glue the fangs to the front.

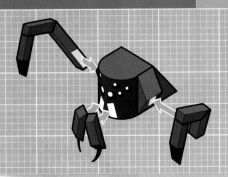

33 Carefully cut out the pieces for the inner chest.

34 Glue the web mounts to the inner chest and glue the webs to the mounts. Glue the microchip bugs to the webs.

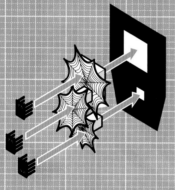

35 Cut, score, and fold the pieces for the upper body. Carefully cut out the spider web pattern on the upper body (1.3).

36 Assemble upper body, gluing the tabs, leaving the back open, and glue on the side, neck, and torso swivels.

37 Glue the inner chest (4.7) to the inner back tabs on 1.3 and then attach back spikes (1.2) to the back flap and glue the upper body shut.

38 Cut, score, and fold the pieces for the torso base.

39 Glue the torso base insert support together and attach the torso base insert. Glue the insert support to the torso base and glue the torso base shut.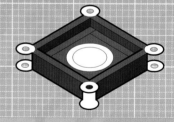

40 Assemble the miniguns. Coil all pieces marked 7.1, 7.2, and 7.3. Roll the pieces marked 7.1 and 7.2 into tubes, and glue closed using the tabs.

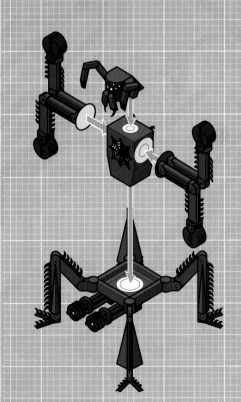

41 Cut out the white circles with a line through the middle in the disks marked 7.4 and 7.7.

42 Glue the disks marked 7.4 together, so that you are left with three disks for each minigun. Glue strip 7.3 to the dog-toothed tabs of the disks marked 7.7.

43 Slide the tubes through the disk holes.

44 Assemble the minigun base, gluing the tabs, and glue swivels to the bases. Glue the miniguns to the swivels.

45 Glue the minigun bases to the torso base.

46 Attach the legs to the torso base, sliding the axle from step 24 through the lower hip in the torso base, then slide through the hip cylinder and through the top hip hole in the torso base. Fan out the tassel-like pieces of the axle, over the hubs of the torse base. Seal this shut with the brown hip hub covers.

47 To complete: Glue the arms to the side swivels on the upper body. Glue the rear head piece to the neck swivel. And finally, glue the torso base to the torso swivel.

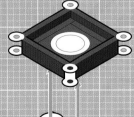

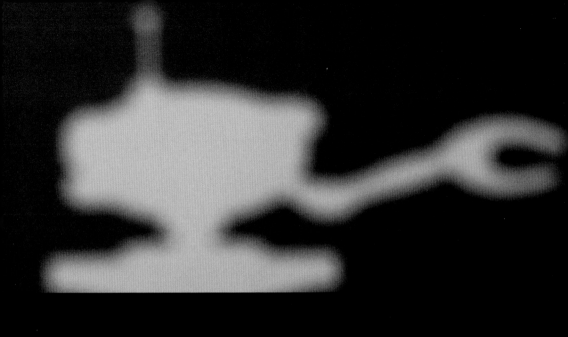

BACKGROUNDS

MECHA CITY

1 Roughly cut around the pieces for the platforms and bases marked 4, 5, and 11 (there should be five groups in total) and glue these to a blank sheet of card. Leave aside to dry.

3 Cut and score the slot keys, marked 3. Fold them along and glue together, then glue the slot keys to the tabs on the back of the background.

2 Choose one of the backgrounds, (either piece 1 or 2) and cut this out. Score along the side tabs, and fold over, then glue down to the back of the image.

4 Cut, score, and fold the pieces for the base and platform plugs, marked 7 and 12, and the pillar connectors, marked 6 and 8.

Mecha City is a noisy place, filled with sounds of humming motors, clanking metal, and the rumble of robots on the move. It is also a safe haven for your mecha models, with fueling stations, lookout perches, and high-rise iron scaffolding.

The Mecha City components can be printed out as many times as you like, so you can create multiple backdrops for your models. Additionally, the background artwork and pillars can be slotted into position in various different places so you can experiment with the basic design—adding extra backdrops, platforms, and bridges.

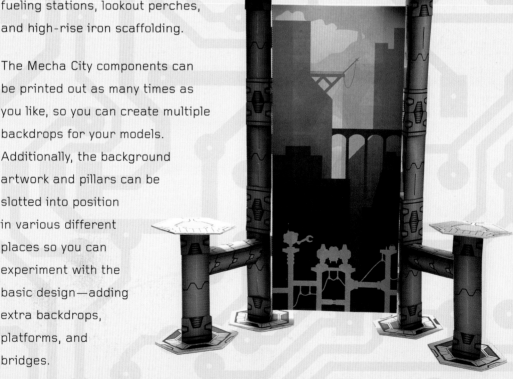

5 Assemble the base and platform plugs by only gluing the end tab to the corresponding end of the plugs. Do not glue the triangular tabs yet. Now repeat the process for the pillar connectors, but here, glue the two small triangular tabs to the inside of the large tab. When all the pillar connectors are assembled, pick up two pillar connector pieces and glue the large triangular tabs of each together so that they are back to back. This will form a complete pillar connector.

6 Cut, score, and fold the pieces for the pillars, marked 13, and beams, marked 14. Also cut through the slots marked with a white line on the pillars.

7 Assemble the pillars, gluing them closed with the end tab.

8 Assemble the beam in the same way. Note that there are no slots to be cut out on the beam.

9 Cut, score, and fold the pieces for the slot keys for the beam, marked 15.

10 Assemble the slot keys by folding in half along the dotted line. Glue the two halves together.

11 Fold the two rectangle tabs on the slot keys, ready to attach to the beam (one key for either end).

12 Carefully glue each tab to the inside of the beam. Make sure that the arrow tabs jut out at the ends and align with the slots in the pillars.

13 Cut out the pillar bases, marked 5, from the extra card. Fold the pieces along the dotted lines and carefully glue together. Cut off any extra white card. The pillar bases should now be four sheets thick.

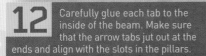

14 Repeat this process for the small platforms, marked 4.

15 Repeat this process for the large platform, marked 11, and glue large platform plugs, marked 12, to the white triangle on the large platform.

16 Now glue the base plugs to the white triangle on the pillar bases, using the three triangular tabs.

17 Glue the platform plugs to the white triangles on the small platforms.

18 To assemble the pillars:
a) Insert one end of the pillar into the pillar connector. Attach another pillar to the other end of the pillar connector.
b) Now insert the other end (the bottom) of the pillar into the base plug.
c) Insert the free end of the second pillar into another connector, insert another pillar on top and insert the platform plug onto the top.
d) Repeat until you have two long pillar structures.
e) Attach another pillar to a pillar base and a platform plug. Repeat until you have two short pillar structures.

19 Now attach the beam to the pillars: Carefully insert the arrow tabs into the pillar slots so that the beam is now attached to the pillar. Ensure that the side of the beam facing upward is a flat edge and not a pointed edge.

20 The beam should be attached to a large pillar structure on one side and a small pillar structure on the other.

21 To assemble the background you have several options: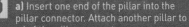
i. Connect all the pillars together and attach the large platform to the top of the tall pillars.
ii. Connect all the pillars together and attach the background of your choice to the tall pillars.
iii. Alternatively, you can print out even more pillars and pillar bases and make two more sets of pillars. You can then attach these to both backgrounds and the large platform base.
Play around with your options; the slots on the pillars mean you can assemble these in any way you please. Think of it as paper building blocks.

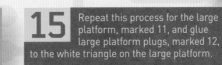
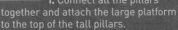

CYBER PORT

The Cyber Port is a platform for your models to be stationed during inter-planetary trips. Able to house six robots at any one time, you can print out and build as many as you like with enough space for a mecha army.

The hexagonal structure allows for six separate platforms to surround the center pillar, but there is nothing to stop you printing extras as the platforms slot neatly into one another and you can expand on the original design.

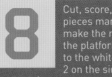

1 Cut, score, and fold parts 1–3. Assemble the little square support structures marked 3, by gluing closed with the end tab.

2 Line up the square supports on part 1B, leaving space between them, so that they are in a square centered around the middle of 1B. Glue in place.

3 Glue the platform sides marked 2 to the tabs on 1B, marked with a red dot.

4 Finally, fold down the tabs of 1A and glue them to the inside of the platform sides, marked 2.

5 Make sure that the numbered side of the platform is opposite the white box on part 2, and is the side that is glued to the main platform structure when assembling the base. Repeat until you have six platforms.

6 Cut, score, and fold the pieces marked 4–6. Assemble this in the same way as the previous platforms.

7 Cut, score, and fold the pieces marked 7–8. Also cut out the interior areas marked with a *. Assemble this in the same way as the previous platforms. Note that this structure does not have the inner square supports of the previous platforms.

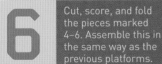

8 Cut, score, and fold the pieces marked 9. These make the mini steps for the platforms. Glue them to the white box on part 2 on the side of the platform (opposite the numbered side on the platform top).

9 Cut, score, and fold the pieces marked 10–13. Also cut out the interior areas marked with a *. Using the dots as a guide, assemble these to make six mini hexagonal structures.

10 Cut, score, and fold the pieces marked 14–15. Using the dots as a guide, glue and assemble these to create a long bar and the tower attachment.

11 To assemble:
i. First glue the platforms (1) to the main platform base (4).
ii. Now insert one end of the long bar into the hole in the part marked 7 and glue the end to the inside of this platform.
iii. Above this, slide on the part marked 10 and then slide on two of the structures marked 11. After this slide on the part marked 13 and then slide on the third part marked 11. Finally slide on the part marked 12; this should only have one hole so that the top is covered. Glue the other end of part 11 to the inside of part 12.
iv. Leaving a gap between parts 12 and 11, glue the part marked 15 to the long bar marked 11.
v. Now slide all the pieces along the bar with even gaps between each.
vi. Finally, glue the platform marked 7 to the top of the platform base marked 4A.

Acknowledgments

Contributor Biographies

Axel Bernal
Model: BOLOBOT

A lifelong fan of papercraft, Axel Bernal is an Industrial Designer with multidisciplinary interests. His work includes toy and furniture design, jewelry, glassmaking, and concept art and set design for movies.

He has participated in expositions in Mexico, Spain, The Netherlands, and Colombia, and teaches glassmaking at Mexico's National University (UNAM).

axelbernal@yahoo.com
www.munmaus.blogspot.com

Josh Buczynski
Models: CHOMPYBOT, MICROBOT, and MECHA CITY

Way back in high school, Josh's first paper model was a dodecahedron. Much later, the popularity of paper models on the Internet provided a great foundation for learning and exploring his own ideas. Years of hobbying around have gone into making poseable paper bots for the sole purpose of covering his desk.

paperposeables.blogspot.com

Elso López
Model: DOGBOT

Elso López was born in Maldonado, Uruguay, in 1980. He has been making scale models since he was a child, and, in 2006, was awarded a specialist diploma in scale modeling. Since then, he has made many models, experimenting with different kinds of materials, as well as cardboard and basic paper. In 2008, he started a blog, where he shares his craft and techniques, including his model of Wall-e, the Disney-Pixar robot, which was awarded the Best Wall-e Model of 2008 by www.wall-ebuilders.com!

He also paints T-shirts, makes woodcraft works, uses fiberglass techniques and builds RC airplanes.

elsoo@hotmail.com
www.elsocraft.blogspot.com

Model construction: Adam Baldwin, Isheeta Mustafi, Nick Rowland, and Adam Smith. **Illustrations:** Peters & Zabransky Ltd. **Photography:** Chris Gatcum. With special thanks to Cláudio Dias of Paper Inside (www.paperinside.com).

Julius Perdana
Model: CYBERBOT, DESTUCTOR, and CYBER PORT

Julius Perdana Putranto is a self-taught graphic designer and 3D modeler of architectural animation. He also works as a web developer. Despite a background in architecture, he began his career as a graphic designer for a printing company in Jakarta, Indonesia, in 2001. Having co-founded two small graphic design companies he now works as a freelance graphic artist.

In 2007, he started up a website, julescrafter.com, a military themed paper model online store, turning his childhood hobby into a money-making scheme. The following year, he created a freebie site, which overlapped his first in popularity. Paper-replika.com is now one of the most popular papercraft sites around.

He is currently preparing to release another papercraft site, called paper-costume.com, which will allow visitors to download costume plans that are entirely made from heavy paper.

www.paper-replika.com

Arif Suseno
Models: BLAZEFIGHTER, CONSTRUCTOR, LIONBOT, and MEDEVAC

Arif Suseno, nicknamed "cerebrave," was born in Jakarta, Indonesia. Having had a childhood filled with many self-made toys, the creations he loved most were his first paper robots. Using only scissors, a ruler, and marker pens he started creating his own paper robot designs.

Now, having embraced the modern digital world and 3D modeling, he creates many paper models, which you can find on his site at www.hobikitkertas.com. His designs are mainly robots, military vehicles, and characters from beloved games.

www.hobikitkertas.com

Kurt Young
Models: SPIDERBOT and TANKBOT

Kurt Young's passion for papercraft dates back to a childhood fascination with origami, but his paper engineering skills also have a more contemporary connection: when he's not putting together paper robots, Kurt repairs and upgrades submarines and aircraft carriers for the US Navy. A huge Transformers fan, Kurt continues to create new paper robot designs, testing his knowledge and skill with each build.